Deceived

God Brought Purpose from My Pain

ENDORSEMENTS

Commanding, intense, insightful, inspirational, motivational. These are words used to describe the book, *Deceived: God Brought Purpose from My Pain*. From the pit of despair to the liberation of her mind, soul, and spirit through her salvation and healing journey, Molly takes the reader through the traumatic events that led up to and follow an abortion decision.

Deceived isn't just about Molly's personal experiences, she introduces the reader to scientific research and tidbits of other testimonies she's heard in her decades of pro-life involvement. The lies and deception about abortion are exposed from a personal, political, and spiritual perspective. This book will minister to the hurting, educate the uninformed, convict hearts, and set ablaze the desire to end abortion and bring forth healing and revival in America.

—**Michele Bachmann**, former US Representative from Minnesota

No one likes to be deceived, much less admit we've been deceived. When the act of deception leads to the death of millions, and the emotional crippling of a society, the truth must be told. In her book, *Deceived: God Brought Purpose from My Pain,* Molly White candidly, openly, and honestly shares the truth about abortion. From her personal experiences with abortion, and the emotional trauma that ensues, to her salvation, healing, and pro-life activism, Molly exposes the lies and deception that brought the legalization of abortion to America. Molly weaves into her testimony, stories from other women and men, research, biblical insights and truths that shines the light on the abortion industry and the legalization of abortion. Readers will be educated, encouraged and inspired to get involved in ending abortion in America.

—**Marjorie Dannenfelser**, President, Susan B. Anthony List

Everybody hates the shedding of innocent blood. It is a demonic attack to legalize killing by abortion. Molly White's book is another major contribution to defeat the enemy. The army of pro-life prayer and action warriors is growing all the time to abolish abortion as the crime against humanity. The ladies of Operation Outcry, like Molly White, who were deceived, are the heroes to lead this army of abolitionist. The truth sets us free.

—**Bert P. Dorenbos**, President Schreeuw om Leven (Cry for Life) Holland and co-founder of the Abolition of Abortion Federation

Deceived: God Brought Purpose from My Pain is the perfect title for Molly White's book. She gives readers an unvarnished glimpse into her troubled life after abortion. We need tools like this book to shine a light on the truth of abortion. Not only for what it does to millions of babies, but also to demonstrate the emotional and sometimes physical torment it inflicts on the mothers and fathers who chose abortion. My prayer is that *Deceived* will minister to those hurting souls.

—**Brad Mattes**, Life Issues Institute, International Right to Life Federation

Molly S. White

The book you are holding in your hand is one woman's candid journey from deception to defilement to denial to depression to destructive behavior and, ultimately, to God's deliverance that set her free. Molly White opens her life up with courage and humility to allow the reader to peer into her innermost being. She writes passionately about her struggles with America's national sin, which has brought national calamity and her personal involvement with the sin and crime of abortion. I recommend you take the journey and prayerfully read *Deceived: God Brought Purpose from My Pain*, especially if you are post-abortive. Perhaps, you too can discover that where sin abounds, much more does God's grace abound (Romans 5:20). We serve a Savior that can take what the enemy of our souls means for harm and turn it to the good to save the lives of many.

—**Rev. Rusty Lee Thomas**, National Director, Operation Save America

Molly White's life story is a powerful testimony of life, death, and life again. Her powerful witness has already changed the world. Learn how you can make a difference against unrighteousness and injustice. No matter how low, how small, or how damaged you think you are.

—**Allan Parker**, President, the Justice Foundation, Operation Outcry, and the Moral Outcry Project

Molly White invites us to understand a vulnerable place in her heart, revealing the pain and sorrow of times past. Many women will find her story aligns with their own and will be encouraged to read of God's amazing grace and love; a love that redeems us and allows us a fresh start, with new opportunity to fulfill His purpose for our lives.

—**Carmen Pate**, podcast host for "Saving Grace," a ministry of Grace School of Theology

Molly White's eloquent testimony is her true commitment to defend life, which is at the risk of being sacrificed on the altar of political correctness. This is a book that contains a lot of common sense and guidance for anyone who wishes to understand one of the challenges faced by women who are victims of abortions. It is a privilege to have met Molly who continues to inspire many people around the world with her real-life experience.

—**Dr. Theresa Okafor**, Director, Foundation for African Cultural Heritage (FACH).

Many people have written documentaries, commentaries, and journals regarding the life and death choices made by women every day. A pregnancy followed by a decision. A choice must be made. Will it be life or death? But it's never that simple. My dear friend and former member of the Texas House of Representatives, Molly White has walked that journey. She made her choices and her life was enveloped with pain and regrets. In her book, *Deceived, God Brought Purpose from My Pain*, she clarifies what is true and unravels the webs of deception, manipulation, and treachery that is the cornerstone of the abortion industry. This is a must read. Thank you, Molly, for your courage and tenacity.

—**Dr. Thomas Schlueter**, Pastor of Prince of Peace House of Prayer, Director of Texas Apostolic Prayer Network

Deceived by Molly White is a riveting, powerful book exposing the lies and rhetoric regarding the greatest crime against humanity in our generation. Get your copy now and be informed.

—**Denise Mountenay**, Canada Silent No More, Together for Life, International Speaker, Author, Human Life Advocate

In cultural issues today, the tension exists between those who acknowledge truth and reality and those who want to color it with their own justifications so that their selfish choices are plausible. In no other field is that more prevalent than the pro-choice issue. Abortionists deny the personhood of the child; they extol the virtue of exercising choice. They relegate consequences to minor annoyances, and they dodge the realities of long-term, and sometimes deadly, consequences to the mother. In this book, Molly White bravely portrays the truthful and painful realities of all the lies perpetrated by the abortion industry. They lied, but not only to Molly, but to thousands of other women who have experienced the same. However, in these tragic circumstances, God's unfathomable mercy and grace are displayed in power. Her story—from death and degradation to wellness and purpose—is attributable to the magnitude of his ability to weave the giant mistakes of our lives into a life-saving mission. It is hope for those grasping for understanding and needing wholeness from a life of despair.

—**Ann Hettinger**, Public Policy Director, Center for the Preservation of American Ideals

Molly White has written a must-read tool for all of us who care about the unborn children and the scars left after abortion. Sharing her personal testimony, Molly's amazing journey exemplifies a broken life transformed into a powerful and passionate proponent of life. Her book compels, equips, and motivates the reader to take action in defense of the defenseless.

—**Sandy Shoshani**, National Director, Be'ad Chaim Association, Jerusalem, Israel.

Realistic. Honest. True. This book is an exposé on several underhanded abortion issues, including giving young girls and women weakened birth control pills so abortion clinics can make more money from the slip-ups. Former state legislator Molly White tells the real story from the viewpoint of one who believed sex was a game, and abortion was just the removal of a tiny speck, so her life could get back to "normal" again. You won't be able to put this book down. It will feel at home on every bookshelf.

—**Edna Ellison, PhD**, award-winning author of *Woman to Woman: Preparing Yourself to Mentor* and *Deeper Still: A Woman's Guide to a Closer Walk with God*

Molly White's book is deeply intimate, raw, and honest. She takes the reader by the hand through the dark valley of her abortion. *Deceived* will speak straight to the hearts of millions of women and men who have suffered through the same heartache. I believe it will give them light and hope.

—**Father Frank Pavone**, Catholic Priest, National Director, Priests for Life, Pastoral Director, Silent No More Awareness, Staten Island, NY

Through this absorbing exposé of abortion and the aftermath in one women's life, one can more fully comprehend the reasons some women end up at abortion clinics, their experience having an abortion, and the devastation abortion brings to their lives. Through Molly's riveting story, we also learn there is hope and healing. I strongly recommend this powerful, in-depth revelation of Molly's story, *Deceived*.

—**Ann LaBrie Olson**, Education Director, Human Life Alliance

Deep personal experiences. Passion. Unwavering commitment. Powerful message. Remarkable resilience. Friendship. These are the characteristics I have come to know in Molly White from battling side by side with her in Texas for two decades. The Molly White story will bless and inspire others to stand boldly for babies in the womb, their moms, and their families.

—**John Pisciotta**, Director of Pro-Life Waco, Creator of the Hometown Pro-Life Action group on Facebook

I have great joy in recommending Molly White's book: *Deceived: God Brought Purpose from My Pain*. The title tells it all: Molly's painful journey as a victim of the lies of the abortion industry to the Truth that sets you free. It is to her great credit that she has recorded this journey and has become an advocate for life.

—**Babette Francis**, National & Overseas Co-Ordinator, Endeavour Forum Inc., Australia

Deceived

God Brought Purpose from My Pain

Molly S. White

ELK LAKE PUBLISHING INC
Plymouth, Massachusetts

Cover and Interior Design: Derinda Babcock
Editor(s): Susan K. Stewart, Deb Haggerty
Author Represented By: Hartline Literary Agency

PUBLISHED BY: Elk Lake Publishing, Inc., 35 Dogwood Drive, Plymouth, MA 02360, 2019

Library Cataloging Data

Names: White, Molly S. (Molly S. White)
Deceived: God Brought Purpose from My Pain / Molly S. White
188p. 23cm × 15cm (9in × 6 in.)
Description: The true story of one woman's abortion experiences that speaks for millions of women.

Identifiers: ISBN-13: 9781951080761 (trade) | 9781951080778 (POD) | 9781951080785 (e-book)
Key Words: Abortion, Grief, Christianity, Healing, Hope, Personal Testimony, Activism
LCCN: 2019953177 Nonfiction

DEDICATION

This book is dedicated to Jesus, who saved, delivered, and healed me; to our Father, God, who has shown me unfailing love and is using this once broken vessel to rescue those being led away to death—to hold back those staggering towards slaughter; to the Holy Spirit who has guided me, taught me, and protected me along the way.

I cannot overlook my Operation Outcry sisters. This book is also dedicated to you. You're the victorious overcomers and, through the power of testimony, many others will be victorious overcomers, too.

TABLE OF CONTENTS

ACKNOWLEDGMENTS

How do I begin showing my gratitude to those who've helped me write my story? This was a labor of love. So many people showed me love by helping me complete the assignment God gave me many years ago. I didn't know the first thing about writing a book, but I had a story that God wanted me to share because it's a story that many women can relate to. A story that is the story of countless others like me. This project has taken more than five years to finish. During this process, I experienced deep spiritual warfare, frustration, roadblocks, and manuscript changes. I felt like I was on an emotional rollercoaster. Now, the journey is completed, and I have many to thank.

I would've never seen this book completed if it hadn't been for my Spanish professor, who was also my pastor, telling me I had a gift for writing. Thank you, Dr. Michael Thomas. If you hadn't said that to me and complimented me on my Spanish writing projects, this book would've never started.

A big thank you goes out to Cecilia Coffman who, in the beginning, read my handwritten story and typed it for me.

Thank you to my dear friend and mentor, Edna Ellison. I met Edna at the first writing conference I ever attended. Your humor, kind spirit, and deep faith endeared me to you. When I picked up the phone and asked you to help me get through the hurdle I was facing, you encouraged me to write my book the way the Lord was leading. Thank you for editing my first manuscript and getting it ready for me to pitch to my publisher. Your prayers, encouragement, kind words, patience, and dedication to my project have been a tremendous blessing to me.

The Lord used many people to encourage me to write my book. Amos Martinez, my dear friend, mentor, spiritual advisor, and supporter never gave up on me. Your steadfastness to keep me encouraged to get it done was just what I needed.

Thank you to my dear friends Denise Mikeska, Dr. Claudette Scott, Mayela Banks, Denise Seibert, and so many others who encouraged me, prayed for me, and insisted I press on to get the book done.

Most of all, I want to thank my family for your patience and your belief in me. My dear husband Ronald. You work so hard to provide for me and our family while I'm out chasing my dreams and doing what the Lord has called me to do. You're the wind beneath my wings and my steady rock in this unsteady world. To my amazing sons Robert and Ty. You've always encouraged me to do things I felt the Lord leading me to do and supported me along the way. You were quick to forgive my terrible mistakes and gave me the confidence I needed to speak for those who cannot speak. To my lovely daughter Natalie—when you were just a child, God showed me your spiritual gifts of discernment and prophecy. You've used your gifts to help me and gently push me to do what I know I'm called to do. You all have loved me when I was broken and wounded. You loved me through my painful healing journey, and you love me know. Your love has carried me through all those things and still carry me through life day to day.

To my devoted parents. When I was young, people often told me I had wonderful parents and how much they admired you. I hate to admit as a child I didn't always see what they saw. As an adult, I see exactly what they saw in you and so much more. Your devotion to your children is unwavering. Your love for each other is a role model for marriage. Your love for your fellow humans is rarely seen in any other people, but is what this world is lacking. And your love for your country and God should make others envious. Thank you for giving me life. Thank you for raising me in a home full of love, opportunity, laughter, and adventure. Thank you for always believing in me. And thank you for loving me even when I was unlovable.

Finally, thank you to my publisher, Deb Haggerty, who was quick to take my project and patiently waited for its completion. And to Susan K. Stewart, my editor. Your patience with my questions, getting my corrections back to you, for the hours of editing and kind words, and for seeing this project through.

May God richly bless all of you for being such a blessing to me.

CHAPTER 1

The Seed Called Choice

"It hurts! It hurts!" I cried out in agony. My body heaved in pain as I clenched the edge of the examining table. The knuckles on my hands turned white. I'd never felt anything so excruciating. I felt as if my guts were being ripped out of my body as the doctor tugged and pulled on the suction tube within me. "Stop," I moaned. "Stop!"

"Shh," said the attendant as she put her hand over my mouth. "You'll scare the girls sitting in the waiting room."

Scare the girls in the waiting room? What do you mean scare them? I'm in terrible misery, and you care about the women in the waiting room? My thoughts instantly flashed back like rewinding a movie to when I arrived at the Women's Health Center of Austin not even an hour earlier. When I opened the door and glanced around the small waiting room, I noticed it was full of women and teens. Some women were accompanied by a man. I saw mothers with their teenage daughters. No one was talking. No one made eye contact with anyone else. I was alone and nervous, not fully convinced to have an abortion. My heart and mind had been in an intense conflict about my choice ever since the doctor in my small-town medical clinic told me abortion was the answer to my unplanned pregnancy.

My mind had been justifying all the reasons I should have the abortion. A medical professional suggested it. They wouldn't suggest anything that was bad for you. It's legal, so "it" can't be a baby yet. I've been dumped by the father. How can I raise a child by myself? Having this abortion will keep me from shaming my parents. At the same time my heart was tugging at me. I didn't understand why my heart was so conflicted. I decided in order to appease my heart, I would ask three important questions before I would agree to go through with the procedure.

I slowly approached the receptionist desk where a middle-aged woman sat looking down. My heart was pounding. My palms were sweating. I took a deep breath and in a low, almost whisper said, "My name is Molly Gosney. I have an appointment at 10 a.m."

"Yes, I see you here on the list. You'll need to take a seat and fill out these forms while you wait." The woman handed me some papers.

"Before I do, I have some questions I would like to ask." My voice trembled, my stomach in knots. "I'm about nine or ten weeks along. What does my baby look like?" Without blinking an eye and a stone-cold look on her face, she grabbed her pen and tapped the tip on a piece of paper making a small, black dot.

She looked at me, tugged on the collar of the white medical jacket she was wearing, then pointed at the piece of paper, and with a firm, unwavering voice said, "It's just a teeny, tiny clump of cells no bigger than this dot."

I sensed a bit of relief. Be still heart, it isn't even formed yet. I prodded her again, "When I called in to make my appointment, I was told anesthesia cost extra. Is the procedure very painful?"

The woman looked at me with a reassuring smile. "It's not any worse than the cramping you feel when you start your period."

My nerves lessened a little more. I shifted my weight onto one leg and leaned on the counter that divided the two of us. I took another breath and asked my last question, "Are there any risks involved with having an abortion?"

Without hesitation she responded, "None whatsoever. Why, at your age, abortion is safer than childbirth. Just imagine, you'll be able to get your life all back to normal real soon." She pressed the papers towards me, "Now hurry and fill these out, they're about to call your name." An agonizing pang jolted me out of my thoughts back to the reality of what was happening to me.

"Oh! It hurts so bad!" I groaned loudly tossing my head back and forth. Beads of sweat formed on my forehead, my legs in the stirrups of the examining table quivered uncontrollably.

"Shh. I told you. Quiet!"

Being a people-pleaser and hating confrontation, I tried not to moan, but I could not stop crying. My hair and ears were damp with tears that flowed down my cheeks.

"Be still. It will all be over soon," the doctor mumbled gruffly from behind his surgical mask as he continued tugging and pulling. His eyebrows frowned above his steel-gray eyes. The slurping sound of the vacuum respirator was a repulsive noise in my ears. The room began to smell like blood. I glanced down the table and saw a glass specimen jar filling up with blood and clots being suctioned out of my uterus. I turned away, sickened by the sight of such gore. Shock waves ran through my body as I realized a tiny dot of cells wasn't filling up the jar.

I stared at the ceiling, as reality slapped me in the face. Oh my God! What am I doing? My body convulsed. I was being violated, medically raped. A stranger was between my legs invading my body with medical instruments and hurting me with every rough shove and pull of the vacuum. The spasms jolting through my body became suddenly insignificant to the torment now gripping my heart. Horror filled me as I realized this doctor was murdering my child and killing my soul.

"Here are some cookies and orange juice." I could hear a woman's voice, but I don't remember seeing her. I looked down and saw them on a tray in front of me.

"I don't want them," I muttered. Where am I? How did I get here? Who dressed me? I must have passed out or gone into shock from the pain. The woman's voice broke through my conscious again.

"You must eat these before you can leave. You lost a lot of blood and you need the sugar," she said. I was bleeding profusely. I could feel warm blood soaking my pad. My stomach cramped with intense contractions. My thoughts drifted back to the receptionist. She lied to me. If a woman's period felt as agonizing as this abortion, women would have only one period immediately followed by a hysterectomy.

I was dizzy and closed my eyes. After some time passed, I was able to eat a bite and take a sip of the bitter juice. Looking around the room, I saw other young women like me sitting in recliners like mine. The room was eerily quiet, or was the shock affecting my senses? My memory was fuzzy and my ability to grasp reality was blurred. All I wanted was to hurry and leave. I gasped as I started to feel suffocated.

"I am ready to leave," I said to the middle-aged woman attendant who was standing by a counter in the corner of the room.

"Let me see if you are cleared to go," she replied. She stepped out of the recovery room and was gone for what seemed like an eternity. I didn't know the clinic lab had to confirm the abortion was complete before patients could leave. In other words, the "contents of the uterus," as the abortion industry prefers to describe a developing human being and placenta, had to be completely removed. If not, the patient's abortion was incomplete, and they needed another abortion procedure to remove anything left in the uterus or face a deadly infection.

It seemed like an eternity before the woman returned. I tried not to make eye contact with the other women in the room. Heavy blood flowed from me. How am I going to make the hour and a half drive back without overflowing the pad? I heard the door open. The woman appeared.

"You're good to go," she said. Her voice was hard and cold. "Here's an antibiotic. Take these pills three times a day for ten days. And here are some birth control pills. Take one a day so you don't make the same mistake again."

I mused with anger as I grabbed the packages. I know how to take birth control. I have been on them since I was a junior in high school. I had very painful periods, so my mother took me to a doctor who prescribed the pills to alleviate cramping and heavy bleeding. I remember her telling me on the way home that those pills were not my walking papers to have sex. Little did she know I already was. I guess I didn't take them correctly, and that's why I got pregnant. This time I would take them like clockwork.

The nurse interrupted my thoughts, "You'll continue to bleed for up to two weeks. If your bleeding gets heavier and looks like you are passing clots, you need to get to a hospital right away."

What? Clots? Hospital? My head couldn't comprehend her words, which rolled out like meaningless blocks on a conveyor belt and were still echoing in my mind as they fell to the ground.

She helped me out of my chair, held onto my arm, and walked with me down a long hallway. Weak from cramping and loss of blood, my legs trembled with every step. She opened a door for me to leave. I staggered into the bright sunlight. Squinting, I looked around and was stunned when I realized I'd been escorted to the back alley behind the abortion clinic. My body was still in shock. I stumbled through the alley as an overwhelming flood of regret, remorse, sadness, and anguish began to surface. I was about to lose control of my emotions. I didn't know how to deal with these raw symptoms of distress, which were about to consume me. I tried to swallow them and regain some type of composure.

I can't believe what I've done. Me, the girl who wanted ten children. The girl who loved babies. How could I be so stupid? I just made the worst mistake I've ever made in my whole life and there's absolutely nothing I can do about it now. Okay, I've made a mistake. I'll just put it behind me and never, ever have another abortion again.

I made my way out of the alley and around the building to the front parking lot where my friend Gene was waiting for me in his pickup truck.

Gene and I had been friends for a couple of years. We met on the phone. His company did business for the company I worked for as a receptionist. He had a deep, pleasant voice. We struck up a friendship right away. After several months of talking on the phone he asked me out. I accepted.

Gene was polite, a true gentleman. He fell in love with me, but I didn't love him. I dated other men. Gene and I remained friends. When I told him I was pregnant, he offered to marry me. I knew he would take good care of me and be a wonderful father. I also knew it wouldn't work. I didn't love him, so I declined. Gene was kind enough to drive me to the abortion clinic.

"Are you okay?" Gene asked as I climbed into the passenger seat. He leaned toward me, patted my hand. His face looked gentle, his brown eyes were soft and tender.

"Yeah," I answered, choking back tears. "I'm. . . I'm okay." Maintaining what composure I had left took every ounce of strength I had. After all, I don't deserve to cry because it was my choice to have the abortion. I'll just mark it up as a really bad decision and put it behind me and move on with getting my life back to normal again. Normal. Isn't that what the doctor said?

We didn't talk on the way home. I just wanted to go home, fall into bed, go to sleep, and never wake up.

Gene suggested he take me to his aunt's house to recuperate, so I would not have to be alone. I asked him not to tell her I had an abortion. When he asked how to explain what was wrong, I said, "Just tell her I'm sick with the flu or something"

When we arrived, his aunt kindly helped me to her guest bedroom. I hardly noticed the furniture or the bedcovers. I was numb and tried not to think. I just wanted to sleep. I dropped my purse on the floor, crawled on the soft bed, and curled up in a fetal position. Gene covered me with a blanket. "I want to be alone, Gene." He got up, patted me on the arm, and walked out of the room.

I slept fitfully the rest of the day and night. The cramping and heavy bleeding continued. I only got up to use the bathroom and take care of myself. Thank God, I have my own bathroom. I don't want anyone seeing me like this. I stayed in bed most of the next day too. I didn't come out of my room, not even to eat. Gene's aunt must have been curious about what was wrong with me. She checked on me from time to time, prepared meals for me, and asked how I was doing through the door. I reassured her I'd be okay soon.

Gene checked on me often and brought my meals before he went to work, during his lunch break, and again when he got off work. He stayed at his aunt's house, sleeping on her couch, even though he lived right next door. I am grateful to him for being there for me.

The following evening, and after a lot of coaxing from Gene, I decided to eat with the family. I didn't talk much during dinner. Gene's aunt and uncle and young cousins chatted and made small talk. I tried to act normal, but I wasn't. I'd never be normal again. I returned to my room after dinner, horrified when I noticed I'd bled through my clothes. Gee, I hope no one noticed. This big spot is so embarrassing.

The date was April 28, 1981. My mom's birthday was April 26, the day I had endured my abortion. On the morning of the 29th, Gene's aunt knocked on my bedroom door. "You have a phone call, Molly. It's your mother," she said through the door.

How did she know how to reach me here? I crawled out of bed and went to the phone. Mom was exuberant as she told me my sister, Jean, had given birth just a few hours earlier. "He is a beautiful, blonde-headed little boy. They named him Jackson," Mom said. I could hear happiness and pride in her voice. She and my dad were already at the hospital in north Texas.

"How much did he weight?" I asked.

"Nine pounds, fifteen ounces," she said.

"Wow, he's huge," I responded. I told her I'd pack immediately and be there as soon as I could. I loved my older sister and was excited to be an aunt. The hospital where my sister delivered Jackson was about a four-hour drive north. Still bleeding and cramping, I was determined to go see them both as quickly as possible.

Arriving at the hospital, I went straight to the information desk to get my sister's room number. I was heading down the corridor trying to find her room when a nurse pushing a bassinet came in my direction. She was just about to pass by me when I stepped in her path. Glancing at the bassinet I asked, "Is that the Fetter baby?"

Looking me over and seeing that I wasn't a threat, she said, "Yes."

I couldn't believe my luck. "I'm his aunt. May I see him?" The nurse stepped aside and allowed me to peer into the bassinet. I looked down and saw the cutest baby I had ever seen. His chubby little body was swaddled in a blue blanket making him look like an overstuffed burrito. I fell in love within an instant. A moment later, I was struck with the reality my baby was dead. I will never be able to hold, nurture, and snuggle the child I once carried. About to be overwhelmed with an explosion of grief, I thanked the nurse who pointed to my sister's room. Instead of going to Jean's room, I ran to the nearest bathroom, stumbled into the last stall, and bolted the door.

"Oh my God, what have I done?" Tears gushed from the well of grief I had suppressed like a geyser bursting from the depths of the ground. The sound of my own moaning and wailing was something I'd never experienced before. Seeing my beautiful nephew was a reality slap in the face. I totally lost control of all the torment, disappointment, tears, and anguish I had successfully repressed since my abortion. I grieved so hard I started to hyperventilate.

I guess the nurse must have mentioned to my sister that she saw me in the hallway. Because when I didn't show up in Jean's room, Mom came looking for me. She found me in the bathroom sobbing uncontrollably.

"Molly, are you in here?" I could hear my mother's voice as she entered the bathroom. I knew she'd heard me. "Molly, is that you?"

I didn't want to come out of the stall.

"Molly, what's the matter? Come out of there."

I fumbled with the handle to open the door. I was hysterical. Mom was shocked when she saw me as I emerged from the stall. Tears streamed down my face—my nose flowed like Niagara Falls. I struggled to breathe. I couldn't look at her.

My crying was uncontrollable. My face was wet. I struggled to breath. I was a mess and couldn't look at my mom.

What's the matter? Is she in complete denial? I just had an abortion. Is she completely clueless of what a traumatic experience I had just been through?

I gasped as I tried to speak, "Baby Jackson … my baby's dead. …" Those were the only words I could utter.

"Your sister just had a baby. She's so happy and is waiting for you. Do you want her to see you like this and ruin this joyous occasion? Get a hold of yourself. Wash up and go see your sister."

As usual, Mom needed to get control of the situation. She snapped me out of my hysteria with a barrage of harsh words and stormed out of the bathroom. Crying was unacceptable in my family. When we were growing up, we were led to believe showing emotions was a sign of weakness. We weren't allowed to cry, at least not for more than a few minutes. I'd only seen my mom cry once in my whole life at a funeral of one of my parents' close friends. I'd sat next to her during the funeral. When I heard her sobbing and saw her wipe tears from her eyes, I was shocked. My heart had ached for her, but I didn't know what to do. I had no idea how to comfort her. We also didn't deal with problems when I was growing up. Instead of confronting conflict, we pretended we didn't have any. Just forget about it and go on was my parents' solution to anything that disturbed us.

Mom had never seen any of her children completely break down, I'm sure she was in shock that day in the hospital bathroom. She was probably thinking of my sister's happiness and didn't want my collapse to spoil the joyous occasion. Who could blame her? I didn't, and I still don't.

At the same time, my world was falling apart. I needed to grieve, to be comforted, and to be consoled. Maybe Mom was trying to maintain control of her own feelings of regret and sorrow over my abortion and seeing me in a meltdown may have been too much for her. Or maybe it was a combination of both. Mom and I never talked about this abortion again. Like all of the problems we encountered through our lives, we stuffed them and tried to act as if nothing was wrong and went on with life like we didn't have a care in the world.

I walked to the sink and looked at myself in the mirror. Puffy, red, swollen eyes looked back at me. Black mascara streaked my face. My nose was swollen and raw from being wiped with toilet paper. My cheeks were flushed. My heart pounded as I tried to steady my breathing. How am I going to not look like I'd been crying? I don't even have any makeup to refresh what my tears washed away.

Splashing cold water on my face would only wash off my makeup, making me look even worse. I grabbed a few paper towels from the dispenser and wet them with cold water and pressed them against my face and eyes. The coolness of the damp towel felt good against my warm face. I stayed in the bathroom as long as I could. When I was certain I could handle myself, and my eyes weren't quite as red and puffy as they had been, I went to see my sister.

Jean was a proud, beautiful mother. She and her husband, Darren, had tried for seven years to get pregnant, and now all the longing and waiting were over. She had a beautiful child to love and hold.

My parents and I stayed with Jean and Darren the first night they came home from the hospital. I was infatuated with my darling nephew and was in on all the action of taking care of him: the first diaper change, the first bath, and putting him down for his nap. I even stayed in the room when Jean nursed him. Late that night, I heard Jackson cry, and I got up to tend to him. I bumped into my sister in the hallway and offered to help. I am sure Jean was surprised to see me up, but she was gracious and let me follow her into the nursery.

Besides changing Jackson's diaper, how could I help to my sister? She nursed him, so why was I up anyway? Why did I feel I had to tend to him at every whimper or waking moment? I can see now I was starting to develop a deep bond to my nephew, but not a healthy aunt-nephew attachment. This was like a "he's-my-baby" kind of attachment. What kept me from completely going overboard and competing with my sister as a mother was that I lived four hours away from them.

Looking back, I can see how this infatuation could have gotten out of hand. Distance didn't stop the close feelings I had and still have for my nephew. I went to see him and my sister as often as possible. I am sure my sister and parents were clueless about the way I was feeling about Jackson, whom they called Jack. I know they had no idea how deeply I was suffering from my abortion decision. As far as I knew, Jean didn't even know about my abortion.

I had to tear myself away from my nephew the next day when it was time for me to head back on the long drive home. I had missed enough work, and it was time to get my life back to normal. I shut down my emotions and locked them deep in my heart just as surely as I had bolted the door that day in the hospital bathroom. I don't remember how I said my goodbyes, or if I cried on my way home, or if I was just numb. All I could think about was how cute my nephew was and that feeling made me yearn to be a mother. Sometime during the drive home, my maternal instincts began to grow.

The desire to have a baby became stronger as time passed. What I needed was to prove to myself I could be a good mother. Having a baby was the only way I could prove it. I'd made a horrible mistake by having an abortion. I thought I could erase all the regret, guilt, and self-loathing through motherhood. However, the months and years following my abortion were radically different from my life before that dreadful day. The seed called choice was planted when I was told by a small-town medical doctor that abortion would make my life get "back to normal." A choice I would've never considered otherwise. Instead, the abortion caused my life to spiral out of control down a long, dark path of self-destruction.

> I call heaven and earth as witnesses against you today, that I have set before you life and death, the blessing and the curse. So choose life in order that you may live, you and your descendants. (Deuteronomy 30:19 NASB)

CHAPTER 2

THE REPLACEMENT BABY

After my abortion, I drank more and tried more drugs without caring what could happen to me. I started going back to the clubs where I had hung out with my friends. Shooting pool was one of my favorite pastimes. We had a pool table at our home in Belton, where I began to love the game. When I attended Texas A&M, I enhanced my abilities as a pool shooter. The Dixie Chicken, a popular beer joint and pool hall near the campus, was my favorite hangout. I spent more time playing pool then studying. It was a lot more fun. I learned from the sharks. They liked me and were always willing to give me advice and let me play them. If you want to be the best, you have to play the best. It didn't take long for me to be considered an ace pool player, but I flunked out of college.

My company transferred me to a small town in south Texas. That's where I met Anthony George, a handsome, dark-eyed, dark-haired roughneck. One night, while shooting pool in a local hall, I glanced across the smoky, dim lit room, and noticed a rugged-looking young man watching me. Don't get me wrong here, there were a lot of men in the pool hall. A lot of good-looking men. This one just happened to catch my attention.

My thoughts were interrupted when the man I was playing missed his shot. I could hear the aggravation in his voice. I turned my attention back to the game and noticed he'd left me in a very good position to finish him off. I made the few shots

I had remaining and called the winning shot. As I was lining up for the kill shot, I heard a deep, smooth voice say, "Mind if I play next?"

Sprawled across the table, I looked up from my aim as the dark-haired hunk laid three quarters on the edge of the table opposite of me. The light from the beer sign hanging above the table gave me a clear view of his face. A smile flashed across his lips as he glanced at me.

My heart fluttered when I gazed into his sparkling eyes. Hello, cutie pie. Come on, Molly, don't get distracted, now. If you mess up this shot, you won't be able to play Mr. Good-looking. I stood up from my aiming position, took a deep breath to settle my fluttering heart. It seemed like all eyes in the pool hall were on me. Time felt like it stood still. No pressure. Molly, relax and do what you know how to do. I pulled the stick back and struck the cue ball. It rolled gently towards the imaginary mark I'd drawn on the eight ball. Click. It made contact with the black ball exactly where I'd aimed. The black ball rolled towards the pocket closely followed by the white, cue ball. I held my breath as I watched the eight ball fall into the pocket I'd called, and the white ball slowly come to a stop on the edge of the hole. I looked up at the man I'd just beat, trying not to smile too big.

"Good game," he said as he put his cue stick back in the rack and walked away.

"You're next," I said, chalking the end of my pool stick and nodding at the mysterious challenger. He looked me up and down, inserted his quarters in the slot, and racked the balls.

I don't know if he's trying to intimidate me, or flirt with me, but I'm not going to let his cute little self distract me. I took my position for the break: CRACK! One, two, three striped balls fell into pockets on the table. I chalked my cue stick again, blew off the extra powder, and blasted one striped ball after another into the pockets until I reached the final shot for the win. I flashed him a grin.

"Eight ball, corner pocket." I tapped my stick on the right corner pocket. I could see the disbelief on the brown-eyed hunk's face in my peripheral vision. It was a difficult shot, but one I had made many times before. I pulled my stick back and hit the cue ball. It glazed the edge of the eight ball causing it to roll down the rim of the table into the pocket. I had just run the table on the dark-haired stranger standing on the other side. I looked at him and gave him as innocent a smile as I could fake.

He laughed, came around the table, reached for my hand and congratulated me. "My name is Anthony George. You're one heck of a pool player. Can I buy you a beer?"

Be still my heart. Anthony led me to a table and pulled out a chair for me. We hit it off immediately. We drank a few beers, talked, and got to know each other. He had a great sense of humor. He made me laugh and that smile. His smile had me hooked from the beginning. Soon we began dating. Our relationship turned intimate in a short time.

Just a few months into my romantic relationship with Anthony, I got pregnant. The second time I conceived while taking the birth control pill. Later, I learned abortion doctors prescribe low dosage birth control pills because of their high failure rate, which in turn leads to more abortions. This time, I was excited about being pregnant. Finally, I can prove to myself that I can be a great mother. I loved Anthony, and I could see us having a happy life together. I couldn't wait to tell him.

"I'm pregnant!" Anthony looked up across the dinner table. He blinked in disbelief.

"Are you sure?"

"Yes, I'm sure. I took a home pregnancy test, and I have symptoms."

"Well. Okay, then. How far along do you think you are?" he asked.

I clearly heard disappointment in his voice but was too excited to let it sink in. "I don't know … about seven weeks or so. What do you think?" I yearned for Anthony to be excited too.

I looked for a happy smile, but I didn't see it.

He was quiet for a few minutes. My heart stopped waiting to hear some kind of encouraging and supportive words.

"We'll work it out."

I felt some relief, yet deep down I knew he was not excited about our pregnancy like I was.

Anthony finished his job in south Texas, and we moved to east Texas, where he was from. After settling into our apartment, Anthony started talking to me about abortion. I couldn't believe it. I even allowed him to make an appointment for me at a clinic in the Dallas area. I don't know why I didn't have the gumption to refuse and close the subject. I wasn't about to have another abortion. I would just have to think of something.

We drove to Dallas and stayed the night with a dear high school friend of mine, Josie. I confided in her, telling her my plan to go to the appointment, but there was no way I would go through with the abortion. She was supportive, offering to go with us or come to get me if he decided to dump me.

Anthony and I didn't talk much that night. My mind was consumed with thinking of ways to get out of this situation. Who knows what he was thinking? Probably how relieved he would be after he skirted his responsibility of being a father.

The next morning, we drove to the clinic located in a multi-story office building. It was a lot nicer than the abortion clinic in Austin. There were pictures of flowers and scenery on the soft-yellow walls, which made the room feel light and airy. Several other couples sat in the waiting area, but no one talked or looked at each other. A television brought a gentle sound into the otherwise quiet waiting room.

After signing in and filling out the paperwork, I sat next to Anthony to wait my turn. I had my plan all worked out in my head. I felt confident about not going through with the abortion but not confident enough to tell Anthony. Though I was angry with him, I didn't have the courage to stand up for myself.

"Molly Gosney. Molly Gosney?" I could hear a woman's voice. I was so deep in thought my name didn't register in my consciousness right away. Anthony nudged me in the ribs. Startled, I looked up to see a woman dressed in a white medical jacket standing by the doorway to the back.

"Molly Gosney?" The woman said again as she looked around the room.

I took a deep breath, looked at Anthony with uncertainty and slowly stood up.

"That's me."

"Please follow me," she said, as she led me down a hallway of rooms.

"Here we are. Take off your clothes and put on this gown. The doctor will be with you in a minute." She left the room closing the door behind her.

I'm not about to get undressed. I mused as I pulled myself up on the examining table. I'll just sit here and get ready to take my stand when the doctor comes in. Within minutes, a tall man with slightly graying hair came in the door followed by the nurse. When I'd had my abortion, I was already lying on the table with my feet in the stirrups before the doctor entered the room. When he did come in, he already wore a surgical mask and didn't look at me or speak to me until he began the abortion procedure.

"Hello, I'm Doctor Hughes. How can I help you today?"

"Look, Doctor, I can tell you one thing. I am not going to have an abortion." The doctor's eyes grew wide, his eyebrows shot upward. He and the nurse exchanged the same look of bewilderment.

"Then why are you here?" he asked.

"Because of the son of a bitch sitting in the waiting room." There it was. The anger I felt toward Anthony just blurted out.

"Well, I see. It looks as if you may be too far along for me to do the procedure anyway. How about going in for a sonogram, and we can talk again afterwards."

I agreed. It can't hurt to have an ultrasound.

The procedure didn't take long. The attendant jellied up my belly, pressed with the ultrasound wand for a few moments and said, "Ok, you're done. Here's a towel. Wipe yourself off, and the nurse will be back to get you in a minute."

That was fast. I never had an ultrasound before. What did she see on the monitor? My thoughts were interrupted by the sound of the nurse's voice. "You can come with me now."

She led me across the hall back to the examining room.

"It looks like you are too far along for an abortion after all," said the doctor when he returned to the examining room looking at my ultrasound images.

He didn't tell me how far along I was, and I didn't ask. He wished me well and left the room. I scooted off the table and left as quickly as possible. I found my way back down the hallway that led to the waiting room. How about that? I'm actually going to leave through the same door I came in, not through the back alley. I felt relieved and confident.

Anthony, on the other hand, raised his eyebrows when he saw me walking through the waiting room towards the door. I wanted out of there as quickly as possible. He got up and followed.

"What's wrong? What happened?"

"I'm too far along. I can't have an abortion!" I never slowed my pace as I headed to the elevator. Anthony was close on my heels, leaning forward to hear me. I'm going to be a mother and there wasn't anything anyone can do to stop me. Well, to be safe, I won't tell my parents right away.

> Be strong and courageous, do not be afraid or tremble at them, for the Lord your God is the one who goes with you. He will not fail you or forsake you. (Deuteronomy 31:6 NASB)

CHAPTER 3

A couple of weeks later, I gathered the nerve to call home and tell my parents I was pregnant. Mom sounded disappointed, but I'm sure the excitement in my voice influenced her to be happy too. She had just lost her father, my beloved grandfather. Maybe my news took her mind off her sadness.

"How far along are you?" she asked

"I'm not sure. Maybe fourteen weeks or so. I have an appointment with an obstetrician this week. Mom, I think I'm going to have twins."

"Twins?" Her voice raised to a higher pitch. "What makes you think that?"

"I don't know. I just got a hunch. I gotta go, Mom. I'll call you after my appointment. I love you."

"I love you too, Molly. Goodbye."

I hung up, feeling another burden lifted off my shoulders. Now my parents know, and I can be at peace.

A funny thing happened to me the next week: One day I could wear my jeans, and the next day, I couldn't even come close to buttoning them. I seemed to have poofed overnight.

As days flew by, Anthony and I finally went to our first doctor appointment. I really liked the friendly doctor. As he listened to the fetal monitor, I blurted out, "I think I'm carrying twins."

He pulled the stethoscope from his ears and looked at me, "Twins? What makes you think that?" He pulled the gown back over my stomach.

"I don't know. Call it women's intuition. Funny thing, though, one day I could wear my regular clothes and the next day my belly just popped out like a can of biscuits that busted through the seams. It was really weird. Is that normal?"

"I don't know about normal, but you do measure bigger than fourteen weeks. I thought I heard two heart beats too." That's all I needed to hear. I was convinced I carried twins. The doctor helped me to a sitting position. "I'd like to schedule an ultrasound. Can you come back next week?"

"Yes, I can." I could feel my cheeks flush with pride.

"I'll get the nurse to make an appointment. You'll have to drink a lot of fluids and hold your bladder before and during the ultrasound. It shouldn't take long though. After that the nurse will reschedule you to come back to see me."

Anthony was waiting for me in his truck. I told him about the ultrasound appointment and the doctor saying he had heard two heartbeats. I couldn't wait to find out.

"Ma'am, you have to finish drinking this before I can start the ultrasound." The technician sounded miffed that I wasn't ready to begin the procedure. The doctor had instructed me to drink about a quart of thick, chalky substance prior to my appointment. There was no way I could drink all that stuff within an hour of my appointment. I carried the remainder of the liquid with me, thinking I could finish it before we started.

"I'm sorry, but I tried," I groaned. "There's no more room inside me." Not only did I feel I was about to pop from being so full of that concoction, but I urgently had to use the bathroom.

"No, you can't go to the bathroom. I need your bladder as full as possible for a clearer image." The technician tried to convince me to finish drinking the stuff, but I explained to her there was no more room.

"Okay, let's give it a try, but if I don't get a clear image you'll will have to drink more," she said.

I got up on the examining table and tried to lie down. What a challenge. I could no longer lie on my back. When I did, I felt as though my air supply was cut off. The young woman agreed to take as many breaks as I needed. She also asked a nurse to bring me a couple of extra pillows, so I wouldn't have to lie flat on my back.

I winced as she squirted cold, gooey jelly all over my protruding belly. With the monitor facing me, she pressed the probe along my belly and watched the image on the screen. "Do you want to know if you are having a boy or a girl?" she said, as she hunted for my baby.

"I think I'm gonna have twins. That is why I'm here. The doctor said he thought he heard two heart beats."

"Well, let's just see. . ." she said, pressing the sensor and searching. "Look, there's your baby." I peered at the monitor to make out the image she saw.

"Here's the head and the body and the heart. Look how fast it's beating. Hear that whooshing noise? That's the heart beating."

I was amazed at the sound of the heartbeat. I had never heard anything more thrilling. I squinted and sat up a little more to get a better view. I could finally make out the image of a tiny little person on the screen. That's amazing. Look at him moving around so fast.

That was the first time I'd ever seen an image of a baby in the womb. I don't even remember studying fetal development in high school, but I was under the impression that ovaries were located in the brain. Believe it or not, I wondered, Wow, how does that egg move down your throat and into your uterus without feeling it? By time the health class was over, my misunderstanding cleared up. A sting of reality pierced my heart as I realized I wasn't carrying a tiny clump of cells. I saw a head, a body, arms, legs, fingers, and toes. I could see the heart beating. My mind instantly went back to my abortion experience. I remembered asking the receptionist What does my baby look like?It's just a tiny blob of cells no bigger than this dot on the paper, she said. She lied to me. I was deceived.

"Here's the other baby." Those words broke through my thoughts. I focused on the screen and saw the image of my second baby.

"I knew it. I just knew it!" My heart pounded as my spirit soared. I felt giddy with excitement. I gazed in amazement at the image of my second baby. I laid back down absorbing the news.

"Uh-oh." Suddenly she thrust me out of my moment of enthusiastic gloating.

"What, what do you mean 'uh-oh'? Are they stuck together? Are they Siamese twins?" My excitement turned to fear.

"No! There's another one in there. Triplets, I see triplets!"

"Triplets?" My heart raced. I couldn't believe it. Never in my wildest dreams would I have thought I'd be carrying triplets. I stared at the ultrasound monitor as the technician revealed the third baby.

"Here is one, here is the other one, and here is the third one. I don't see any more."

"I can't breathe, I can't breathe," I gasped. The woman jumped up and helped me to a sitting position. The shock of having triplets would probably cause most women to lose their breath, but I had just laid on my back too long. Pressure from the weight of my stomach had cut off my air supply. I took another potty break, which gave me a little more time to absorb the news.

I'm going to have three babies. Three! Somehow, I felt as though I was blessed, given another chance, but this time with more than I was expecting. In my mind, I knew there was a god. My maternal grandmother used to sing us songs like "Jesus Loves You" and "I've Got a Home in Glory Land." We attended church a few times growing up, and I went to kindergarten at a Presbyterian Church. I knew of a god; I just didn't know God.

I'm sure the technician was relieved I was happy. We pressed on through the rest of the ultrasound. She had to measure every part of each squirming baby to get her report ready for the doctor. With my drinking the liquidy goo, going to the bathroom, and sitting up often to breathe, it took about two hours.

I glowed all the way out of the examining room, down the hallway, past the nurse's station to the receptionist's desk. I felt I was walking on air. Word must have spread to all the nurses and receptionists because everyone was looking at me and smiling, but no one was smiling more than me.

I glanced towards the waiting room to see if I could spot Anthony. He was nowhere in sight. The receptionist noticed my eyes scanning the room.

"If you're looking for the gentleman who brought you, he stepped outside a few moments ago. Would you like me to get him?" The receptionist smiled at me.

"Yes, that would be nice."

She stepped from behind the counter and walked to the door. When she pushed the door open, Anthony walked in. He looked at me with questioning eyes. He must have been sitting on pins and needles while waiting for hours to hear the results of whether he was going to be the father of twins or not. I didn't say a word to him. I just held up three fingers and gave him a smile. I don't know if Anthony smiled or not. Looking back, I realize I was too self-absorbed to notice, but our relationship wasn't the same from that moment on.

———— ❧ ————

I could hear my phone ringing from my apartment as soon as I'd gone down two flights of stairs to talk to my neighbors. It hadn't been more than thirty minutes after we returned from the doctor's office. I knew it had to be my mom. I ran up the stairs, skipping every other one, to reach the phone before the caller gave-up. In those days, we had landlines—phones connected to a cord inserted into a phone jack in the wall. I was out of breath and hurting, but that didn't stop me. I reached for the receiver, "Hello," I panted.

"Hi, Molly, it's Mom. Why are you out of breath?"

"Because I just ran up the stairs." Even though I was barely into my second trimester of pregnancy, the pressure on my lower abdomen caused shooting pains throughout my pelvis area. I didn't bother telling my mother.

"Well, what's the news? Are you having twins?"

"No, Mom," I panted. "I'm not having twins." I lowered my voice to a sad tone. I really wanted to surprise her with the news.

"Well, maybe next time," she said, trying to comfort me. In the background, I could hear the mumbled voices of her coworkers at the local travel agency.

"She's not having twins." Mom relayed the news. I could hear them sigh with disappointment and express their sympathy. Everything is going as planned. She's about to get the surprise of her life.

"Mom, are you sitting down?" I said in the saddest voice I could muster.

"Yes," I could hear her excitement turn to concern.

"I'm not having twins … I'm having … triplets!"

Her scream was so loud I pulled the phone away from my ear.

"Triplets!" Her voice trailed off as she turned to share the news. "I can't believe it. Triplets. Are you feeling okay? How far along are you? What did the doctor say? Are they boys or girls or both?" The questions came as rapid as machine gun rounds.

"I'm fine Mom. I'm sixteen weeks, they're all boys, and the doctor told me to stay in bed with my feet propped up. Yeah, right."

"All boys. I can't wait to tell your father. You better do as the doctor says. I'm so happy, Molly. This is wonderful news. No one in our family has ever had triplets. You stay in touch, and I will be checking on you, okay? I love you."

Mom couldn't wait to hang up the phone. I'm sure the switchboards were lit up the rest of the day as my mother called everyone she knew in Bell County. No doubt all her clients at the travel agency would hear about it too. She was one happy and proud grandmother, even facing the fact that her daughter was single and pregnant.

I must have been caught up in all the excitement and not seen that Anthony was the only one who wasn't happy about my pregnancy. Our relationship deteriorated to the point that my parents soon came and took me back to their home to live for the rest of my pregnancy. Anthony would call occasionally. He and I decided we needed to get married before the babies were born. He drove down one Friday afternoon, and we went to a Justice of the Peace in Waco and got married. We stayed at my parents' house the remainder of the weekend. Anthony left on Sunday. I only saw him one other time before the babies were born.

Carrying triplets was quite the experience. By my sixth month, I could no longer fit behind the steering wheel of a car. By my seventh month, I was already bigger than a full-term pregnancy. Even though I was in great spirits and felt good, I couldn't stand for very long, walk very far, or sleep very well. I quit going out in public during my eighth month because people would gawk at me. I stayed home and enjoyed having company. Preparing the nursery was a lot of fun.

As each day passed, the babies continued to grow and my discomfort level increased. Getting in and out of the bathtub was impossible, so I used my parents' shower because it had a built-in bench I could sit on. I could only fit into one large robe, which I wore all the time. My uterus grew so big, I could place a full-size dinner plate on my belly and use it like a table. I had to. I couldn't get close to an actual table. Eating was difficult too. I felt like my stomach had been shoved up under my throat. As soon as I took a couple of bites of food, I felt full.

On one occasion, Jean and Benjamin came to visit my parents. She insisted I go to the movie E.T. with her. Boy, was that a mistake. The movie was so loud the babies began to kick and squirm and move. It felt like they were turning flips inside me. My belly heaved, rolled, and contorted. I couldn't breathe. I leaned over and whispered in Jean's ear, "I've got to get out of here. The babies don't like the noise. You and Benj finish watching the movie. I'll wait in the lobby." I grabbed the seat in front of me, heaved my body out of the chair, and waddled out of the dark theatre. Once the doors closed behind me, and I was out in the lobby, the babies settled down, quit moving, and I could breathe normally again.

I was so anxious to have these babies, time seemed to have stopped. My doctor thought I'd go into premature labor and hoped I would make it to twenty-eight weeks. Twenty-eight weeks came and passed. Thirty-six weeks arrived and still no babies. I called my doctor when I started experiencing Braxton Hicks contractions at thirty-eight weeks. He didn't seem too concerned since they'd come and go. He told me if I hadn't gone into labor by my due date, January 18, to come see him. Still no babies, so on the due date my grandmother drove me to the appointment.

The staff at the clinic always seemed happy to see me. Each time I came in they were amazed how much bigger I had grown. I think I could've been a Guinness Book of World Record holder for largest pregnant woman, measuring more than sixty-four inches around. I waddled back to Dr. Macey's examining room hoping he would tell me I was dilating and labor would come soon.

"Well, it could be tomorrow or two weeks from now," said Dr. Macey as he helped me sit up from the examining table.

"Two weeks? I cannot go another day. I'm miserable. I can't eat, stand, or sleep. If I get any bigger, I'm afraid I'll explode. Can't we take them?" I moaned.

"Would you like to be induced?"

"Yes! Can we do it today?"

"No, not today. I'll schedule you for tomorrow morning. Go home and get a good night's sleep and check into the hospital at six a.m. We'll get everything going first thing." Dr. Macey smiled as he left the room. My grandmother and I were thrilled. Finally, after nine long months I will be meeting my baby boys pretty soon.

Darkness was all around me. I felt far away and alone in space. I didn't know where I was. I just knew I needed to try and find my way out of oblivion. Moments of consciousness would come and go like the flashes of a strobe light in a dark room. During one flash, a memory sparked in my mind. Yes, that's it. My babies. I had my babies. All my family and friends are here waiting to hear the news. I must be coming out of the anesthesia they used to put me to sleep for the cesarean. I need to wake up.

I tried with no success to open my eyes. I could hear the sound of voices nearby. They must be the nurses I hear talking. I struggled to speak. With all the force I could muster in my state of semi-consciousness, I muttered, "How are my babies?"

"Shh, shh." I heard one of the nurses try to silence the other. Footsteps approached my bed. I felt a presence near my head. I struggled to open my eyes, but I couldn't. "The doctor will be here shortly," a soft, woman's voice broke the silence.

Shh, shh? What does she mean, 'shh, shh'"? A doctor will be here soon? Why can't she tell me about my babies? Like the deafening sounds of warning alarms blaring through neighborhoods causing all those in hearing distance to become alert of their surroundings, all my bodily systems were blaring to alertness. My maternal instincts kicked in, and I began fighting the remains of the anesthesia to return to full consciousness.

"How are my babies?" I demanded to know.

"The doctor will be in shortly to speak to you, Mrs. George."

I barely recognized the nurse was speaking to me. I hadn't been Mrs. George for very long. "Mrs. George?" I was able to force my eyes open to see Dr. Macey and a pediatrician standing next to my bed.

"How are my babies?" I asked again, fighting to regain full consciousness.

"I'm sorry, but two of your children were stillborn. Would you like to see them?" His words hit me like a sword piercing my heart.

"No, no!" I cried aloud. I can't believe this. Tears of grief flooded my eyes. Trying to make sense of what I was hearing, my mind instantly played a recording of the events of the day. I was induced into labor early that morning, labor progressed steadily, the nurse came in to check the heart beats of the babies. She said she could only hear one heartbeat. She got Dr. Macey. He came in, took the fetal monitor, and pressed and probed until he heard three heartbeats. Then the anesthesiologist came in and talked about whether I wanted to remain awake during delivery or be put to sleep. That was it. The nurse knew something was wrong, but the doctors covered it up. I began to sob harder. Shockwaves rippled through my body like a bolt of lightning running through an electrical system. I could feel my life draining from my body. I felt death about to consume me. I wanted to die.

Dr. Macey put his hand on my arm. "Mrs. George, you have a beautiful son who is crying for you in the nursery."

A son, I have a son, and he is crying for his mother. Those words literally saved my life. I'd been ready to give in to death. The pain of grief had almost overtaken me. Hearing that my baby son, my only survivor, was crying for me gave me the will to live. I must see my baby.

I was still crying and in shock as an attendant wheeled me out of the recovery area toward a private room. My body began to shake so violently. I felt I'd shake myself off the gurney as it moved down the corridor. The attendant would have passed the nursery completely if my mother had not blocked him from passing.

"Stop. She needs to see her baby." my mother demanded.

I looked at her. Her eyes were red and swollen. I knew she was trying hard not to cry. "Look," she said. "Look in the nursery window." I turned to see a nurse standing there, holding the most precious baby boy I'd ever seen. Yes, a baby who was even more adorable than my nephew. He had dark hair and big cheeks, and he was crying.

"O how sweet." The joy I felt did not deter the overwhelming grief I was experiencing. In just a few short minutes, my life had been turned upside down. The joy of having triplets turned into unimaginable sorrow. I was devastated to have delivered two dead babies but, at the same time, happy to have one. The deepest hurt came when I thought this god I had heard about had punished me in the worst possible way he could punish a woman—by taking two of my children. I felt I'd just been spiked like a glass football and completely shattered.

Now, I'm the mother of three dead babies. One by my own choice, and two I couldn't even bring into the world alive.

Grief is a powerful emotion. It's consuming and unpredictable. It controls you making you feel powerless and weak, but it also brings healing if "done properly." God's word says, "Weeping may endureth for a night, but joy cometh in the morning" (Psalm 30:5b KJV). I believe my grief was exacerbated by the unresolved grief over my abortion. I didn't allow myself to cry then, and I wasn't allowed to cry now. As the weeks passed, I suppressed my sorrow and tried to be a good mother. It wasn't easy. I filed for divorce shortly after the funeral. Anthony wanted to give up custody. I'm sure it was the stress of the financial obligation. At the time, I thought it would be best. I couldn't bear the thought of him having partial custody and taking Nathan away to Tyler during his visitations. I continued living with my parents for the first year after Nathan's birth. They were a huge help taking care of him, and they became very attached.

Nathan and I moved out of my parent's home a year later. I found an apartment nearby and a job at a local radio station. It was a bittersweet move. I was grateful for my parents and all the help they gave to me. They helped me raise Nathan and loved him deeply. I looked forward to my new life, but I was still deeply wounded. Life is never the same after abortion. I was changed forever, emotionally, spiritually, psychologically, and physically. I didn't realize or recognize the extent and depth of the damage to my mind, soul, and spirit. The unresolved issues I was experiencing continued leading me on a downward spiral of self-destruction.

> The spirit of a man can endure his sickness, but as for a broken spirit who can endure it? (Proverbs 18:14 NASB)

CHAPTER 4

Being a single parent was challenging. Working and making a home for me and Nathan kept me busy. But I couldn't wait to get back in the social scene, to be around my friends, and to party, which included drinking and smoking marijuana again. It was an escape from the losses and pain.

It was different this time. No longer was I a carefree individual, I was more emotionally damaged. On the social side, I struggled with how I'd explain to someone I was a single mother, who'd lost two of my triplets, and was still in the recuperating process. How could I expect a man to care, much less want anything to do with me?

I enjoyed my job at the local radio station and my coworkers, especially a cute redhead who worked in another department. I nicknamed him Red. He had a great sense of humor and was so darn cute. Red mustered up the nerve to ask me on a date.

Being asked out helped me regain some self-esteem. At least he wasn't someone who had hit on me at the club. We had a wonderful evening, laughing, joking, and talking about what we liked. We had quite a bit in common. He wasn't threatened that I was a single mother, because he was a single father. Maybe I was still emotionally unstable, not capable of making healthy decisions, or maybe I had missed male companionship the past two years, but we ended up sleeping together on our first date. Obviously, the need to feel some human closeness that night outweighed any good judgment. Worst of all, I wasn't on birth control.

Red and I never went out again. Talk about feeling rejected and used. How could I've been so stupid and gullible? Really, was sex all he wanted? Why couldn't I see through that? I thought he was a nice young man. I would see Red at work from time to time, and we would talk, but it was more like small talk. I started to realize he was avoiding me. I was heartbroken. Then came a missed period. Oh my god, I can't be pregnant! Give it a few more days. Maybe I'm just stressed out. A few days came and went. I had a sick feeling I was pregnant, and sure enough, the home pregnancy test showed I was. Pregnant? I'm pregnant. How could you be so stupid. Really? One time, the first time I've been with a man in over a year, and I get pregnant. What are Mom and Dad going to say? Surely, they'll support me. They did with the triplets and now with Nathan. You better call them and tell them and get it over with.

"Hello, Mom. What're you up to today?"

"Hi, Molly. I'm just piddling around the house today. How's Nathan doing?"

"He's fine. Listen, Mom I need to tell you something."

"Oh, is everything ok?" I could hear concern in her voice.

"Well, not exactly. Mom, I don't know how to tell you this, but I'm pregnant."

"What? Are you serious?"

"Yes, Mom, I'm serious."

"Molly, how could you? How could you do this to me and your father?"

Mom was not happy. I could hear her voice crack as she held back tears, but not her anger. She hung up the phone on me and left me staring into the receiver in disbelief. Who could blame her for being upset and angry? I certainly didn't. I knew she would be. I had already put her through two terrible relationships and two pregnancies, now this. All the feelings of guilt, rejection, shame, and grief started surfacing. In my fragile, emotional state, I needed support from the only people I had in my life—my parents. We had made it through my last pregnancy and relationship. I thought this would be another hurdle we would have to get over together. Not so.

That evening my parents came over to my apartment. I was sitting on the living room floor changing Nathan's diaper when they charged in the front door. I had no idea what was in store.

"How could you do this to us? You're pregnant again by a different man? What are our friends going to say? You're not going to embarrass us like this again. You're not having this baby. You can't have this baby. If you don't have an abortion, we won't support you anymore. Do you hear me? We're through." my mother wailed.

I burst into tears. "I can't have another abortion. I've already been through that. I just buried two babies." I sobbed. The thought of going through the pain and grief again was too much for me to bear.

"If you don't have an abortion, your father and I will not help you and Nathan anymore," Mother insisted.

"You're going to do what your mother says. Do you hear me, Molly? We won't help you, not one penny, nothing." My dad said through clenched teeth. I believed him.

I'm facing an ultimatum. Either I have an abortion or face raising my son and another baby all alone. My parents had been great help to me. When I couldn't leave work in time, Dad picked up my son from day care. They watched him when I went out. They helped me financially if I needed it. What would I do without their help?

Mom kept pressuring and hounding me.

"I need an answer right now. I'm not leaving here until you agree."

I was sinking into despair. Deep down inside I could feel rage starting to build as the pressure from my parents continued.

"Fine. I'll have an abortion." I pulled my son close and sobbed. "I'm not making the arrangements, and I'm not paying for it." I looked up, tears streaming down my face. "I'll have an abortion, but the blood will be on your hands," I screamed. The tears of sadness turned to tears of anger.

My mother was appeased. "Fine then. We'll take care of everything, but you need to talk to that boy and get him to pay for it," Mother demanded. She and Dad left as I sat on the floor holding my son and crying.

The next day, my mother called. "I made an appointment to talk to a doctor in Temple. We have an appointment on Thursday."

The following day at work I looked for Red and found him in the engineering room. Red looked startled when I entered the room. "I need to talk to you. Can you meet me out back in a few minutes?"

"What do you want to talk about?" He looked put out because I had barged into his workspace.

"Can we talk in private? Out back. Now? Please?" I walked out of the room.

The pleading look on my face and sound in my voice must have done the job. Within a couple of minutes, the back door to the station opened and Red walked out into the bright sunlight.

"Pregnant? Are you sure?" Red faced me. Confusion and disbelief covered his face. "I have a daughter. I don't need this right now."

"What do you mean, you don't need this. What about me? I was a one-night stand, and now I'm pregnant. My parents want me to have an abortion, and they want you to pay for it."

"I'm not paying for an abortion."

"Then are you going to help me raise this baby?"

"No, no! I can't believe this is happening to me. I don't want to have anything to do with this. Nothing. Do you hear me? Nothing." Red stormed back in the building. My heart sank in despair. Deep down inside, I hoped he would tell me not to have the abortion, and he would help me raise the baby. My hopes were too high. I was all alone facing something I didn't want to do.

Rejection is painful. Abandonment is frightening. I already suffered from those and now, faced them again. I felt I had no other choice, but it was a choice I didn't want.

In Texas, February weather can be bitter cold one day, then warm like spring the next. February 13 was a cold, bitter day. The cold air stung my face as I walked out of my apartment to my mother's car. I was numb, but not from the cold. Numb from my feelings and the reality of where I was going, and what I was about to do.

I was disgusted when she told me we were going to the same clinic where Dr. Macey practiced. I can't believe it. I'm going to the same clinic that delivered my babies to have this baby terminated? If I had known they did abortions in the first place, I would've never gone there.

Mom must have been feeling guilty. She kept talking to me about the reasons why I needed to have the abortion while we drove to the clinic. "Molly, you do realize this is the best thing you can do. How can you raise two babies on your own? Think about your future. Do you think a man will want to marry a woman who has two children by two different men?"

My mind tuned her out. All I could hear was a soft murmur coming from her mouth as my mind drifted elsewhere. Good mothers don't deliver dead babies, and good mothers don't kill their babies.

When we arrived at the doctor's office, I had to check in. It was the most awkward experience I've ever had. The staff knew me. I tried not to make eye contact, and I certainly didn't carry on a conversation with them. I sat next to my mother while we waited to be called back. I just looked down at my hands folded on my lap.

"Ms. Gosney" (I'd taken back my maiden name after I divorced Anthony). I got up, and Mom and I followed the nurse back to the doctor's office.

"Have a seat. Doctor Kiltz will be with you shortly." I don't remember his name, but this is how I always thought of him. Mom and I did not speak as we sat in the leather chairs, which matched the doctor's desk. Dr. Kiltz was one of Dr. Macey's business partners in the clinic. I'd never met him or seen him before.

A few minutes later, the doctor came in, introduced himself, and sat in his chair. Mom did all the talking. "You understand don't you, Doctor Kiltz?" My mother tried to sound convincing with all her reasons I needed the abortion. I just sat in the chair next to her and looked down at my hands clasped on my lap. "Yes, I understand," Kiltz replied empathetically. "I can start the procedure today. She'll have to come back tomorrow for me to complete the process."

A two-day procedure? Why is he doing a two-day procedure? I wasn't as far along with my first abortion and it only took one day. Anger and frustration churned in the pit of my heart. Ugh, hello! Don't you see me sitting here? The two talked as if

44

I weren't even in the room. I was there physically, but certainly not emotionally.

Doctor Kiltz never talked to me. He never asked me any questions. I was a grown woman, almost twenty-seven years old, and both my mother and the doctor treated me as if I were a teenager. I didn't once look up during their discussion. I was so codependent I didn't have the nerve to stand up to my parents. I was too emotionally weak to fight for myself and my baby. Fear of abandonment and rejection were the driving factors for me even being there. That should have been a clue for this medical professional; I didn't agree to or want to have an abortion. He didn't even ask me. Dr. Kiltz spoke to Mom, "I'll call the nurse, and she'll come take Molly to my examining room. Mrs. Gosney, you can wait in the waiting room. It won't take long," he said as he pushed a call button from his desk.

He stood up, shook my mother's hand, and walked out the door. A nurse came and escorted me into an examining room.

I walked down the familiar halls. I knew all the nurses. These women watched me progress during my pregnancy with the triplets. We laughed and joked with each other at each visit. After the babies' birth, the staff was kind and sympathetic.

This time, none of the nurses looked at me or spoke when I walked by. I felt as though they all knew why I was there. I was embarrassed. I wanted to hide. I felt in a daze. Just going through the motions without any emotion, following along like a sheep, just as I had done with my first abortion.

"Get undressed and put this gown on. I'll be back with the doctor in a few minutes." The young nurse's voice snapped me out of my thoughts. She handed me the gown and left me standing in the examining room. I felt the stirring of anger. I felt the grip of frustration. I slowly got undressed and wrapped the gown snuggly around my torso, climbing up on the familiar examining table with my arms and legs crossed in a protective gesture. I heard a knock on the door. The nurse reentered the room. "The doctor will be here in a minute. Lie back on the table and put your feet in the stirrups," she instructed.

Doctor Kiltz entered the room and sat on the short chair on wheels at the foot of the table. My mind started experiencing flashbacks. Having my feet in stirrups brought back terrible memories and the feelings associated with them.

"Relax now. I'm going to insert laminaria. This will dilate your cervix," he instructed in a dry, unemotional tone. I didn't know at the time laminaria, a kelp species, is used in obstetrics to dilate the cervix and induce labor. I lay there staring at the ceiling. Flashbacks of my abortion experience popped in my mind: the bright lights, my feet in stirrups, feeling vulnerable, and my body being violated, again. Suddenly, pain brought me back into the present. "Ouch, that hurts!" I could feel the pressure and stretching as he forced the speculum into my cervix prying it open. Kiltz's voice came from behind the sheet, "Just relax. I'm almost done."

The nurse stepped closer to me. "Take a few shallow breaths. It will be all over soon." I winced when I felt him stuffing cold, moist seaweed inside me. Is this a dream? A terrible, terrible dream? What am I doing here?

"There, I'm all done." Kiltz got up, walked over to the sink, removed his rubber gloves, and washed his hands. "I'll see you in the morning," he said as he left the room. The nurse helped me sit up. "Take these two extra strength acetaminophens and keep taking them every four hours until you come back tomorrow. You'll feel some discomfort. The acetaminophen will help take the edge off. You can get dressed. We've scheduled you to come back at seven a.m. Don't eat or drink anything after ten p.m. tonight." The nurse rattled off instructions before she left the room.

I got off the table. I felt my body react with a sharp pain to the internal invasion. As I was getting dressed and thinking about what had just happened to me, a volcanic rumble of the suppressed anger began to erupt. "Nooooo!" I groaned and began to scream. "No! I can't do this!" I lost it. I lost all control of the anger and frustration I'd tried hard to keep stuffed inside. People all over the clinic could hear the echoes of my screams. It didn't take long for the nurse to return. She stormed into the room.

"Ms. Gosney, what's the matter? What's going on?"

"Get that doctor back in here, now!" I demanded. "I do not want to have an abortion. I never wanted to have this abortion! My mother wants me to, but I don't. Get him back in here and tell him to take this stuff out of me!" I was uncontrollable. The nurse was shocked and looked afraid. She left the room closing the door behind her. Within seconds, she came back in with Doctor Kiltz in tow. I was spewing with anger, pacing the floor like a caged animal.

"What's the matter, Ms. Gosney?" he asked calmly.

What's the matter? What in the hell does he think is the matter? "I … don't … want … to have … an abortion!" I was breathing heavily, fighting back tears. "I never wanted to have this abortion. I've already had an abortion and just buried two babies and have a little boy at home. I can't go through with this. Take it out!" I demanded. I wanted him to immediately remove the laminaria and stop what he had started.

"Ms. Gosney, I can't take it out now. If I do, I risk damaging your cervix, and you'll end up miscarrying."

His words hit me like water dousing a fire. My heart slumped in defeat. All the hope I had to end this nightmare was dashed. I felt all alone. No one offered to help me. The doctor offered none. I didn't know at the time I could have sought medical help somewhere else. I didn't even know I should. When I was growing up, my parents not only demanded obedience without questioning, they also instilled in us that we should always trust and submit to those in a position of authority. I had no reason not to trust doctors, even though all my pregnancy outcomes were very traumatizing. Dr. Kiltz didn't offer to turn from an abortionist to an obstetrician to help me save my baby. He was more interested in the cold hard cash he was about to receive for the procedure.

The doctor and nurse left the room. I stood there all alone, shaking and heaving with emotion. I didn't want to leave. How can I face the nurses? I'm a wreck, and I'm sure I look like death warmed over. What will the people in the waiting room think when they see me? I don't want to face my mother either.

When I mustered enough strength to move, I opened the door and walked toward the waiting room. The hallway and nurses' stations were empty. I didn't notice anyone behind the receptionist's desk. I guessed no one wanted to face me.

I passed through the lobby right by my mother and out the door. She got up and followed me to her car. I slumped into the passenger seat, weak from the whole ordeal. We headed back to my parents' house where I stayed the night. My parents had decided my mother would take me to my first appointment while my dad watched Nathan. On the following day, my dad would take me, and my mother would watch him. I guess it was the easier for my mother. In my mother's era, birth control wasn't even legal. It wasn't socially or morally acceptable especially with the Christian community.

"Molly, this is something that has to be done." She tried to reassure me I was doing the right thing or was trying to convince herself. I tuned her out and withdrew into nothingness, the black hole that was opening up in my soul.

Mom and I arrived back home by mid-morning. The miserable morning turned into a horrible afternoon that progressed into a worse evening. The laminaria was working. My cervix was cramping and throbbing as it was slowly being forced open. The painkillers barely relieved the pain. I withdrew to my room early in the day. I had to be alone. I didn't trust my feelings. The cold, bitter winter day matched the coldness and bitterness forming in my heart.

Even though I was crazy about my son, the sight of him was a haunting reminder of what I was about to do. The more I thought about the abortion, the more I decided it wasn't going to happen. I'm not going through with this. I don't want to have an abortion. I swore I would never have another abortion. How could I allow my parents to pressure me into this? That does it. When I go back tomorrow, I'll tell Doctor Kiltz that I'm not having the abortion. I did it before, I can do it again. I felt more confident and determined once I resolved I wasn't going to go through with it. My night was filled with sleep interrupted by bouts of pain. It was the worst night I ever had.

"Molly, it's time to get up. Dad is ready." My mother's voice woke me from a shallow sleep. I could hear my father in the kitchen talking to Nathan. He had just turned two in January, and my parents adored him. They had bonded quite deeply. Dad must be feeding him breakfast. That's my job, but today I don't feel like it. Hurry and get dressed and leave before Nathan knows you're awake. I didn't have the strength to face my adorable baby before I headed off to the death camp. I wanted to leave before he saw me. Nathan was definitely a mama's boy and didn't like to be separated from me. Once I was gone, he would settle down and play with my mom.

I didn't want to speak to my mother, but I had to. "I'm up. I'll be out in a little while. Tell Dad I'll meet him downstairs."

I put on my clothes, went to the bathroom to freshen up, and slowly descended the stairs. Dad was waiting for me when I appeared on the stair landing. I walked outside and got in his car. I left with a resolve that I wasn't going to go through with the abortion. I did it once before and I can do it again. I thought.

Dad and I didn't say a word on the drive to the clinic. We pulled into the parking lot, I got out and went in the door. Dad followed me. As I sat in the lobby, I noticed the Valentine decorations adorning the walls. Streamers of hearts were hanging from the receptionist area. A big bouquet of roses sat on the counter. The scene was almost surreal. Love and hearts were displayed everywhere, and in the back babies were being killed. How sickening. Nausea swept over me. Contractions snapped my thoughts back to reality. The pain grew more intense as time passed. I was miserable and couldn't wait for this stuff to be removed from my body.

Finally, a nurse called my name. I got up and followed her to a room I had never seen before. I didn't like the looks of it. An examining table with stirrups protruded from the wall. I recognized an ultrasound monitor by the table, and a tray with surgical tools laid out on a towel. I diverted my eyes and refocused on what I was going to tell Kiltz.

"Ms. Gosney, you'll need to get undressed and get up on the table," said the nurse as she handed me a gown. "The doctor and I will be back shortly." She closed the door behind her. My heart was pounding. Cold chills ran down my spine as I looked around the procedure room. I recognized the glass jar apparatus I'd seen during my first abortion. The medical instruments lying on a tray next to the examining table made me want to vomit. I turned away and faced the door. I didn't change. I wasn't going to have an abortion. A few minutes passed, and I heard the familiar knock on the door followed by the entrance of the nurse and doctor. They were shocked to still see me dressed and standing where I was left.

"Ms. Gosney, why aren't you in your gown"? The nurse was obviously flustered because I wasn't ready. I didn't respond to her. Instead, I looked right at the doctor.

"Doctor Kiltz, I'm not going to go through with the abortion. I told you yesterday I never wanted this abortion. I already had an abortion, I've buried two babies, and I have a little boy at home. I can't go through another abortion."

The doctor looked at me sternly, "Ms. Gosney, I already told you it's too risky. You've already fully dilated, and you'll miscarry. You have to finish the procedure. It's too late."

His words hit me like a baseball bat to the stomach knocking the breath out of me. I was stunned. Maybe he doesn't understand how I feel.

"Dr. Kiltz, I don't want to have the abortion." I began to cry. I could feel hysteria surfacing. I began to panic.

"Ms. Gosney. You don't have any other choice."

I couldn't breathe. I couldn't believe this was happening to me. I felt like an animal caught in a snare, a tight noose around my neck. I didn't know at that time I could challenge the doctor or leave and go straight to an emergency room to try to save my baby. I didn't know Kiltz was lying to me. I expected him to be a doctor and do what he could to help me and my baby.

"Come on, Ms. Gosney, let's get that gown on, the doctor will come back in a few minutes."

All I remember of that dreadful day is I had an abortion. Dr. Kiltz used some type of anesthesia on me, so I don't remember the procedure. I don't remember getting undressed or dressed. My parents and I never talked about this abortion after that day. I guess we thought we could bury our memories and our emotions and continue through life as if we were perfectly normal. What I do remember when I left the clinic that Valentine's Day in 1985 is I left dead to my emotions. Dead to my feelings. Dead to my memories. I was dead in a living woman's body.

> But she who gives herself to wanton pleasure is dead even while she lives. (1 Timothy 5:6 NASB)

CHAPTER 5

WHEN NORMAL ISN'T NORMAL

Raising Nathan was a joy, but being a single mother was difficult especially as an emotionally damaged mother. One minute, I couldn't be separated from Nathan. The next, I was running from him and the traumatic memories of losing two of my babies. Giving birth to dead babies was another trauma stacked upon the trauma of my abortions. Feelings of guilt and of being a failure grew. Unresolved grief intensified. I lived in a fog of confusion, sadness, regret, self-loathing, and anger. In the midst of the fog, I tried to find my way through the haze of dysfunctional feelings to love, care for, and provide for my son. He deserved that, and I needed to prove to myself I could be a "good" mother.

My life became reckless and careless after my first abortion. I used drugs and alcohol to numb the pain from the trauma of the abortion. But I also worked and did fun things Nathan and I enjoyed, but I was in a constant state of self-destruction.

After my second abortion, I was numb. I completely shut down my feelings and erased the memory from my mind just to cope. I was ignorant, naïve, and uniformed when I had my first abortion. My second one was different. I knew what was going to happen. I knew my baby was developing, not a tiny blob of tissue.

This time, I went through stages of hating men, using them, and then dumping them just like men had done to me. Even though I was very sociable, maintained a polite, fun-loving manner, and made friends easily, I had anger issues. With one little touch on a trigger button, I could chew someone up— usually a man—and spit him out, leaving him in a puddle of shame and humiliation. The trigger was usually feeling like I was disrespected or a having a conversation with someone who thought abortion was bad or, even worse, a sin. The topic would set me off, and I'd go on a tirade about women's rights, our bodies, our choice, and man's irresponsibility.

My pregnancy with the triplets changed everything. No more drinking, doing drugs, or partying. After Nathan's birth, I tried to focus on being a good mother amid my deep grief. Still, I would go out on the weekends and drink and, on occasion, smoke marijuana. The only feeling I had was anger. I wanted to be a good mother, and I tried.

One day, I got another phone call from Gene. He called me often and even came to visit me and Nathan from time to time. I knew Gene loved me, and he loved Nathan. This time, the call was more than a "how are you and Nathan doing." Gene asked me to marry him. Without hesitation I said, "yes." That was the wrong answer. I thought I could make a marriage work and provide a father figure to my son, even when I didn't love Gene. That plus other issues caused our marriage to end after just a few months.

After divorcing him, I met a very special man.

I looked forward to going dancing on weekends. My friends and I frequented a local dance hall and club. I'd lost a lot of weight, so I looked and felt great. One night as I was sitting with my friends, I noticed a cowboy standing alone sipping on a beer. I was always attracted to cowboys, but most of them were known to be wanderers, with the tendency to avoid commitment or settling down. This particular cowboy caught my attention, and I wanted to check him out. I got up from the table and pranced by him, hoping he'd notice me and engage in a conversation. He didn't.

At a closer look, I was not disappointed. He wore a straw cowboy hat, creased in the popular bull-rider style with the side brim wider and squared across the front. His mustache grew down along the sides of his mouth. He was the cutest thing I had ever seen. He seemed composed, confident, and secure in who he was. I was immediately attracted to him.

My first attempt of getting noticed failed, but I wasn't about to give up. I returned to my table. I began to plot ways of getting his attention without being brazen and forward. I was still an old-fashioned girl who didn't ask men to dance, call them on the phone, or ask them to go out with me. What was a girl to do? He didn't even glance at me when I walked by him.

"Merle, do you see that cowboy standing across the room?" I asked my best friend sitting across the table from me.

Merle looked over her shoulder, her eyes scanning the room. "Which one?" she asked. "There are dozens of cowboys over there."

"The cute one standing alone holding a beer. Do you know him?"

"No, but he is cute," she turned to me and smiled.

"Yeah. I wonder how I can meet him?"

Merle's husband, Jeff, and several other couples were sitting with us. Everyone was laughing and cutting up when I noticed the cute cowboy following a taller cowboy walking towards our table. My heart skipped a beat, and I nudged Merle with my foot to draw her attention to them. To my surprise, the taller cowboy knew some people at my table and started talking. I tried not to stare at the cute cowboy who had gotten my attention. After a few minutes, a popular country song started to play, and couples started to leave the table to dance. Only a couple of girls remained at the table, me being one of them, with the cute cowboy standing there alone. My heart fluttered. I really wanted to dance with him, but I wasn't about to ask him. Come on, Cutie Pie. Ask me to dance. I tried not to be obvious that I was waiting, hoping he'd ask me. I don't know if it was my smiling at him and glancing at the dance floor or sighing heavily, but finally I got a response.

"Would you like to dance?" he asked slowly, holding his hand out towards me.

"I'd love to," I said, as I jumped up, trying not to appear thrilled he had asked.

I melted into his arms as he pulled me close to his muscular body. We danced cheek to cheek, my favorite way of dancing. He was a great dancer with a smooth style. He led me around the floor weaving in and around other couples in the crowded space. His two-step had a nice, slight dip at the knee on the second step. We danced the whole song before we even introduced ourselves.

"What's your name?" he asked as he escorted me off the floor.

"Molly, Molly Gosney. What's yours?" I asked, smiling at him.

"Ronald White."

"It's nice to meet you, Ronald. Thank you for the dance."

That was it. He had just captured my heart. My mind had other thoughts. Don't go there, Molly. He's a cowboy, and he'll break your heart. Oh, be quiet. It doesn't hurt to dance with a cute cowboy, especially this one. He fits me perfectly as a dance partner, and he's so darn handsome. On top of that, he looks great in his jeans, boots, and hat. I give him my lioness growl of approval—grrrr.

I decided this time I wasn't going to listen to my brain and all the reasons I should avoid getting to know him. I was going with my heart. I had never felt like this before. We danced several more times, then the evening was over.

I went back to the dance club the next weekend, and he wasn't there. The following week I arrived at the club and began looking around to see if I could spot Ronald. I sat in an elevated area of the club for a better view of the room. My eyes scanned the entire space like a laser beam. There he is. Heart be still. I noticed Ronald talking to another woman, and my heart wasn't going to have any of that nonsense. I strolled over to where the two were talking.

"Hi, Ronald." I said, as I nudged right in between the two of them. We started chatting, and the other woman walked away. We danced the night away. With each dance, our bodies moved in unison, perfecting each movement as we became accustomed to each other's rhythm. With each country song, Ronald added a little romantic twist to his dance moves. I didn't miss a single change, because I was glued to him. I found myself falling in love with every step, and I was starting to feel he was attracted to me. After the club closed, Ronald took me for a midnight breakfast at Denny's. He brought me back to the club to get my car afterwards. We ended up sitting in his truck all night talking until the sun came up.

I had never believed in love at first sight, but it was happening to me. Ronald seemed so grounded, so strong, with a great personality. He was a quiet man, but when he spoke, it was either funny or wise. He reminded me of my beloved grandfather, who died when I was pregnant with the triplets.

As I got to know Ronald, I learned he was divorced and had a son the same age as Nathan. He told me his visitation was every other weekend. I realized why I hadn't seen him every weekend at the club. When he had his son, he spent all his time with the boy. I really respected that relationship and thought to myself That's the kind of man I need. Someone who is dedicated to his own children. What I didn't see was he was hurting from his divorce and not confident in himself or in trusting another relationship.

I pursued a relationship with Ronald. With every bit of courage I could muster, I even called him at his mother's house. I'd never called a guy before. At least not one who I was pursuing. I invited him to watch a football game at my apartment. He accepted. When the evening was done, he asked me out on a date for dinner and dancing. Ronald and I became one on the dance floor. We were a great dancing couple. He enjoyed playing pool, too, but I beat him every time. We decided dancing was more enjoyable for both of us.

We continued dating and enjoying each other's company. Ronald was a gentleman. His mannerisms certainly debunked all my preconceived thoughts about cowboys. Polite, respectful, a man of his word, and honorable. His personality and humor were charming and endearing.

Ronald had roots in Bell County. I needed someone with roots. Military families like mine didn't establish roots because we moved so often. Both my parents were born and raised in Texas, and my father was stationed in the state many times at various locations. My father is a fourth-generation Texan. My mother is at least a fifth-generation Texan and part Cherokee. We returned to Texas for vacations centered around our yearly family reunion near Junction, the town where my father and his brothers were born and raised.

I loved being around my cousins who were also born and raised in the small towns near my ancestors' homestead. They played a huge role in my love for Texas and the western way of life. They even taught me to dance. Part of the fun during our family reunions was the Saturday night dance at the local dance hall. All my cousins, aunts, and uncles went dancing, kids and all. What wonderful memories! Meeting and dancing with Ronald made me feel connected to my childhood.

Ronald was a true Texan. I, on the other hand, was a Texan wannabee. I wanted to be the country girl who loved to ride horses (which I did, and I'd had a horse since I was in high school), hunt, fish, and wear boots and jeans. While I loved those things, I was also worldly. I had traveled extensively all around the United States and abroad when my father was an Army officer, enjoying privileges most people never have. My mother was a very strong lady, determined her children would experience things she and my father never had the opportunity to experience when they were growing up. Mom was a socialite. She considered manners and proper etiquette of huge importance in our lives. My siblings and I could dine with heads of nations, attend social events or military functions, and behave in ways that made my mom and dad proud. We could also be rough and act up. We just didn't do much of that in front of my parents.

Ronald and I were total opposites in personality and lifestyles, but we had some things in common. Ronald was a dedicated family man, and he loved to hunt and fish. So did I. I think doing those things together attracted Ronald to me. Ronald and I continued dating—eventually he moved in with me. Our kids never knew we were sleeping together. When Nathan woke up, he would find Ronald sleeping on the couch. When Ty spent the night, he always saw Ronald sleeping on the couch.

Nathan and Ty became instant best friends the moment they met. They were six and five. Like Ronald and me, the boys were polar opposites. Ty was an energetic, tough little dude with light brown hair and blue eyes. Though he was short like his mother and father, he made up in speed what he lacked in height. He loved hunting and fishing.

Nathan was a laid-back, easy-going kid, not as outdoorsy as Ty. Nathan was taller by a head with dark brown hair and eyes, who loved team sports rather than hunting and fishing. Nathan was more artsy, and he loved to laugh and make people laugh. Despite their polar differences, the boys became best friends immediately. They enjoyed each other immensely, played well together, and loved being with each other. Because both of them got along well, we had a great time when we did things with them.

On December 24, 1988, Ronald and I were sitting on the couch relaxing after attending his family's Christmas Eve get together. I noticed he was acting kind of fidgety and nervous. This was totally uncharacteristic of him. Then I noticed something bulging out of his shirt pocket. Curiosity got the best of me.

"What's that in your pocket?" I asked as I reached over to take a look. Ronald intercepted my hand before I could get to the pocket on his shirt.

"Nothing."

"Nothing? How can it be nothing when it is bulging out of your pocket?" I deliberately started to tease him.

"Oh, come on. Tell me what it is." I pressed in towards him as if I were going to reach for his pocket again.

"Quit," Ronald commanded as he covered his pocket with his hand.

"Fine. Don't tell me. You sure are acting strange. What's the matter?" I asked. Always the thinker, Ronald was not the kind of man who just spit out what he wanted to say. If I interrupted him while he was talking, his thoughts would be thrown off, and he needed time to recompose them. In earlier encounters, I had frustrated him enough he often refused to finish what he was trying to say.

On this occasion, after an awkward moment of silence, he reached in his pocket and pulled out a ring box. My eyes got big, and my heart swelled with anticipation.

"Here," he said as he handed me the box.

"What's this?" I asked as I opened it up and saw a diamond ring. My jaw dropped.

"You know what it is."

"I can see it's a ring. Is it a Christmas present?"

"No."

"Then what is it?"

I regretted interrupting his plan for proposing to me—down on one knee expressing his deep love for me and asking me to marry him. The romantic side of me wished I had kept silent. I knew Ronald wasn't a romantic kind of guy—at least not in words. He can show the real romance in his heart from time to time, especially through special occasion cards.

I pressed him again, "What's it for? A promise ring? A gift? What?"

"You know."

"Is it an engagement ring?"

"Yes."

"Are you asking me to marry you?"

"I guess."

I could see Ronald was as nervous as a dog going to the veterinarian. I threw my arms around him and kissed him passionately.

"Yes, yes, yes! I'll marry you!"

We snuggled on the couch that evening. I was so happy. I'm going to marry a man I love. Nathan will have a father. I will have the family life I've always wanted.

"Ronald, when do you want to get married?"

"I don't know."

I got up and went into my kitchen, grabbed my calendar off the wall and plopped back on the couch next to Ronald. I flipped through each month as we tried to find the perfect time to get married. We settled on June 3, 1989.

That night I couldn't sleep. I laid snuggled next to the man I wanted to spend the rest of my life with and started thinking about my abortions. Fear and dread crept into my heart. Are you going to keep the abortions a dark secret from the man you love for the rest of your life? I started to have an internal argument between my mind and heart like I did on my way to my first abortion appointment. If you tell him, he may be so disgusted that you did such a thing he'll leave you, but if you don't tell him you'll never know if he really loves you. The internal struggle was intense. My heart pounded with anxiety. I had to know, though. I had to know if Ronald's love was unconditional. Would he still love me even though I had killed two of my children? I decided I needed to tell him my deep dark secret and, if he didn't leave me, then I'd know without a shadow of doubt that he was devoted to me. I nudged him.

"Are you awake?"

"Uh-huh," he mumbled.

"I need to tell you something," I whispered.

Ronald patted my back. "What?"

My heart began to pound with anxiety. I took a deep breath and with every bit of strength I had I whispered, "I had an abortion years ago. Actually, I had two abortions."

There. It was out. I lay there, my head on his chest, listening to his heart beat, waiting for his response. Silence. My mind was going berserk. Does he hate me? Is he going to leave me? Does he think I am a tramp? What is he thinking? Why won't he speak to me?

Ronald never said a word. His action said it all. He pulled me close to him and hugged me tight until we fell asleep. That was good enough for me. I felt a weight lift off my shoulders. If he didn't leave me over that confession, then he must truly love me.

We had a small wedding at a pavilion that overlooked Belton Lake. I didn't feel I deserved a full-scale wedding with a fancy wedding dress at a church with a catered reception and all the bells and whistles my two sisters had enjoyed. My parents were not crazy about the idea of me marrying this cowboy. I had two failed marriages under my belt. How could I ask or even plan the wedding of my dreams with a history like mine?

Thank goodness for my wonderfully talented mother-in-law to be, Emma. Even though she was suffering from the late stages of muscular dystrophy, she managed to make my wedding dress, cake, and bouquet. Merle was my maid of honor, and Ronald's best friend, Jay, was the best man. Both the boys were our ring bearers. With close family and friends by our side, Ronald and I married under an old oak tree next to the pavilion overlooking the lake where we loved to fish.

Though we spent our honeymoon night in our apartment, I tried to make it as romantic as possible. The following month, we took a little honeymoon-style trip when Ronald could take time off work. Because my new husband loved to fish and hadn't been on a vacation of any sort in a long time, we spent a few days on a fishing trip to Del Rio, Texas. Even though we caught a lot of fish, and enjoyed our sweet time together, it wasn't my ideal honeymoon. I think Ronald understood my sacrifice, because ever since, he has allowed me to choose how and where we will spend each anniversary.

Marrying Ronald, I knew I had everything the world had to offer that I needed: a home, a husband I loved, two great kids, and a good job. I should be happy, right? I should be back to normal, right? Not so.

> When you were dead in your sins and in the uncircumcision of your flesh, God made you alive with Christ. He forgave us all our sins. (Colossians 2:13 NIV)

CHAPTER 6

As newlyweds, Ronald and I tried to make our blended family into one. It was challenging. The process was complicated because I was also suffering from depression. At first, I blamed feeling "blue" on cloudy or rainy weather. Then feelings got worse during fall months and around Christmas. Gradually, I started feeling depressed most of the time. My emotional well-being got so bad, I began having ideas about suicide.

My thoughts of suicide grew to an almost uncontrollable impulse. Driving home from work, I'd often think about ramming my car head-on into a tree. The only thing that kept me from following through was the idea of leaving my precious son and the man I loved. I just couldn't do it. Yet my depression continued. I got to the point where I couldn't listen to the news, sad music, or sad television shows. I had to avoid anything tragic because I was afraid it would send me over the edge.

I was busy being a mother of preteen boys and a wife. At that same time, I worked as a supervisor for a home health agency, working with elderly clients. I loved my job because I loved visiting elderly people and providing the individual care needed so they could live in their own homes. Most of all, I loved talking to them and listening to their stories about life when they were young and growing up. Sometimes, I would forget I was working because I loved the socialization and the clients so much. However, it was difficult trying to balance the jobs of wife, mother, and supervisor while dealing with the symptoms of depression.

On one particular day, I visited one of my favorite clients, an elderly black woman, to see if her current home health service was still fulfilling her needs. Her sister-in-law was visiting her at the time. As we sat and talked in her living room, I could hear the news on the television in the background. A reporter talked about a tragic event, which caught my attention. I made a comment about it to the two women: "More bad news. Why don't they ever report on anything that is good?"

The sister-in-law piped in with a conversation about a man named Jesus who, she said, is the Good News. She didn't stop there. She continued talking about Jesus, and how much she loved him but, most importantly, how much he loved us. I was mesmerized, turning my head to look more closely at her. The more she talked about him and who he was, the more I was drawn to what she was saying. A powerful love seemed to emanate from her as she spoke about the Savior of the world. I couldn't take my eyes off her as she shared with me.

This woman had no idea who I was. She had no idea of my emotional state much less my spiritual state. She was just expressing her love for Jesus and his love for us. Like a moth attracted to a bright light, I was attracted to the love I saw coming from her, drawn by the love of Christ himself, who was wooing me through this stranger. I felt an unusual warmth and a spark of joy deep in my heart as I leaned closer to her, almost hypnotized by her tender words and spirit. Love poured out of this woman's eyes and face—a love I'd never experienced before. A love that can't be denied. A love that captivated every ounce of my being. To this day, I can't remember what this woman looked like, but I know what Jesus looks like. I saw him in her as she was praising him.

After she finished, she got up, said goodbye and left. My thoughts were suddenly forced back to my client. I was a little sad she had gone. I hurried and finished my routine assessment with my client, gave her a hug goodbye, and rushed out to my car, looking around to see if I could see where this woman had gone. I knew she must had walked to visit my client because no other vehicle was in the driveway. I glanced all around. I couldn't see her anywhere. I drove around the block looking for her but never saw her again.

Something changed inside me that day. I received a glimmer of hope. Hope I didn't know I desperately needed. My heart skipped a beat. It seemed I was feeling something lovely, clean, and appealing. Something that called me to her Savior. I'd tried everything the world had to offer to be happy, and yet I was miserable. Maybe this Jesus was the way. I went home after work and waited eagerly for Ronald to get home. I couldn't wait to tell him about my experience. Finally, he walked in the door.

"Honey, we need to go to church," I said bluntly. Ronald looked at me, one eyebrow cocked upwards, the other eyebrow squinted downwards. His lips tightened. I realized I had completely shocked him with the statement because we were accustomed to going to the dance halls or fishing on the weekends. Going to church was the farthest thing from our minds.

After a moment of silence for the initial shock to wear off, Ronald responded, "Oh yeah? What makes you think that?"

"I met this woman today who told me all about Jesus. I'd like to go to church and learn more about him."

My wonderful husband agreed to take me. "My friend Mike Randolph is a cowboy preacher. I heard he has Sunday services in the parking lot of the western wear store in town. I'll take you there this Sunday."

"That's wonderful. Thank you, Honey." I hugged and kissed Ronald. For the first time in a long time, I felt excitement quickening. I actually looked forward to something. That night in bed my thoughts turned back to when I was a young child. Memories of my grandmother singing songs to us grandkids, like "Jesus Loves Me" and "I've Got a Home in Glory Land," came to mind. I remembered going to kindergarten at a Presbyterian Church, and a few times my parents had taken us to church on Easter and Christmas. I couldn't wait until Sunday.

"Come on, boys, hurry up. We're going to church this morning. Get your shoes on so we can get in the car." I rushed around the house trying to get the boys ready. Ronald was up and dressed in one of his nice western shirts and boots. (He always looked handsome, and when he cleaned up, I'd give him my approval signal: Grrr!)

We drove downtown to an outdoor makeshift church where Pastor Mike greeted us. We spoke to some other folks we knew and sat next to Mike's mother, Pansy. I don't remember the sermon, but I do remember the invitation to ask Jesus in our hearts. I prayed silently in my seat, Jesus, please forgive me of my sins and come into my heart. Even that sin, Jesus (referring to my unnamed sin, the abortions). I felt wonderful after that brief prayer. My heart was overflowing with relief. When the service was over, Mike's mother approached us and invited us to the church she attended in town, Belton Assembly of God. We agreed to attend the following Sunday.

I could hardly wait for the following Sunday to come around. When we arrived at the church, many nice people greeted us. Pansy found us in the foyer and invited us to sit with her. Instead, we preferred to sit in the back row. The music was great, the preacher gave a powerful message, there were lots of verbal "amens" and "hallelujahs." Occasionally, someone would say something in a weird sounding language or utterance. Ronald and I looked at each other as if to say, "What the heck?" The preacher wrapped up his message with an appeal to those who wanted to surrender their lives to Jesus and invite him into their heart.

"For we have all sinned and fallen short of the Glory of God. For God so loved the world that he gave his only begotten son, Jesus, so that anyone who believes in him shall not perish but have eternal life. No man can enter heaven without the atoning blood of Jesus and the forgiveness of sins. Jesus is the way, the truth, and the life, the Savior of the world. If you would like to receive Jesus as your Savior, I invite you to come forward and I will pray with you."

That's all it took. I was sitting in the middle of the back row, feeling an overwhelming desire to go forward. More than a desire—I was led by some force I'd never experienced before. I elbowed my way out of the middle of the back row, practically running down the aisle and into the arms of the man who represented Jesus. In my normal state, I would have never gone in front of a crowd of people. Never! I didn't even notice the hundreds of people in the room. The preacher laid his hands on my shoulders and asked, "How can I pray for you?"

"I would like to ask Jesus into my heart."

The pastor led me through the sinner's prayer. When he got to one part about repenting for my sins, I thought, *Forgive me even for those, Jesus.* Just as I'd done the weekend before, I wanted to remind Jesus to forgive me for my abortions.

The pastor and I finished praying, and something miraculous happened to me immediately. I opened my eyes and saw color. I glanced around the altar amazed at the beautiful colors of the room. No, I wasn't color blind. It's just I'd lived in depression for so long that my world appeared grey all the time. Depression was my normal.

After receiving Christ as my Lord and Savior, I instantly felt a heavy weight lift off my shoulders. I had no idea I was carrying such a load of guilt from my sins. That day I thought I could walk on air. I was also instantly delivered from smoking, drinking, listening to certain music, and watching soap operas. My life changed radically after just a few moments of prayer. Maybe my life will finally get back to normal. Not so.

Our family started going to church on a regular basis. I was baptized shortly afterward. We got involved in Sunday school, the boys in children's church, and I in women's Bible studies. I hungered for the Word so much I wanted the Holy Spirit to unzip me like a bag and just pour his Word in as fast as he could. I loved reading and studying the Bible and being mentored by the strong Christian women who befriended me. I grew rapidly in my newfound faith. It seemed like my dark days were over.

Ronald didn't grow as I did. He went with me and the boys to church, but he resisted going forward to pray to receive Jesus. He even resisted when I preached to him at home. After several months of trying to urge Ronald forward, the Lord impressed upon me to back off. Well, more like a command to leave him alone. The Spirit of the Lord reminded me no one hounded me into a relationship with him, and he loved Ronald and would take care of him without my help. I felt a little insulted, but I listened and obeyed.

Ronald and I spent about a year at Belton Assembly of God. We made great friends as we attended every time the door was opened. The boys really enjoyed going to church and participating in all the activities for children. My conversion helped me make it through the difficult job of balancing a blended family, work, and church responsibilities. I began to realize I could not do it all. Everyone only got a piece of me. My employer, my husband, my kids, and my church. It was weighing on me more and more. I realized I couldn't do all four very successfully, and my family suffered the most. Something had to give. I decided I wanted to quit my job. One night after dinner, I broke the news to Ronald.

"Honey, I have something I need to talk to you about."

Ronald looked up from the table where we had just finished our dinner. "Oh, yeah? What?"

"Well, I'm having a hard time juggling being a wife, mother, and employee, along with church service. I'm being pulled in too many directions, and I'm not able to give 100% to any of them. Everyone only gets a piece of me so, I decided that either you need to go, the kids need to go, or my job needs to go. Which do you prefer?"

I still laugh when I think about the stunned look on his face when I broke the surprise to him. One eyebrow cocked upwards, the other downwards. His lips were tight, and he gave me the look. He might be a man of few words, but his facial expressions speak volumes. What could he say? I knew he or the kids leaving wasn't a practical option, so the only logical choice was for me to quit my job. Ronald pondered my proposition. After what seemed like an eternity had passed mulling over the options, he reluctantly agreed I could quit my job. I had no second thoughts. No hesitation. The next day I gave my two weeks' notice. Now that I don't have the stress of a full-time job, I'm sure I'll start to feel normal again.

> The Lord is slow to anger and abundant in lovingkindness, forgiving iniquity and transgression. (Numbers 14:18 NASB)

CHAPTER 7

BURIED FEELINGS NEVER DIE

I saw the same look of disbelief and surprise when I talked to him about having another baby as when I presented Ronald with the options of either leaving him, the kids, or quitting my job. I still felt I hadn't finished having children. As a child, I wanted ten children. I had only one child and my maternal instinct wasn't satisfied. I wanted another baby. I wanted Ronald's baby. It took some convincing, but finally Ronald agreed.

We didn't get pregnant as soon as I was hoping. Wouldn't you know, when I didn't plan on getting pregnant I did very easily? Now I'm trying, and it wasn't happening as quickly as I'd hoped. Finally, months later, I had all the signs I was pregnant. I bought a home pregnancy test, took it, and watched closely as a thin blue line began to appear. I'm pregnant, thank you, Jesus! You've answered my prayers and given me my heart's desire. Praise the Lord! I couldn't wait to tell Ronald.

I could hear the rumble of the diesel engine coming down the street towards our house. I jumped on the couch and peered out the plate glass window. I could see his truck pulling into our driveway. With the pregnancy test in my hands, I waited for him by the front door. Ronald walked in all hot and sweaty from working out in the heat all day. I threw my arms around his neck and gave him a big hug and kiss.

"Yuk, you're all sweaty," I said as I pulled away from him. "I got something for you."

Ronald smiled at me, "What?"

I opened my clenched fist and revealed the pregnancy test. "Here." Ronald looked at it for a moment and looked at me. He gave me a smile of approval. "I'm pregnant. Isn't it wonderful?" Ronald hugged me. I knew he wasn't nearly as excited as I was. I think he just gave in to me because he knew how much I wanted another baby. He never showed it though. The next day I made an appointment with an obstetrician, who confirmed my pregnancy. I couldn't wait to get home and tell Ronald and the boys.

I greeted Ronald as he walked in the front door with the usual kiss and hug. "How was your day?" I asked smiling from ear to ear.

Ronald looked down at me and cocked his right eyebrow up.

"It's confirmed. I'm pregnant."

A big smile burst forth from his face as he hugged me close. "That's good; that's real good." A man of few words, what Ronald said meant a lot to me.

"We'll tell Nathan during dinner and Ty when he comes Wednesday afternoon. Does that sound good to you?"

Ronald nodded in approval. I headed to the kitchen to prepare dinner. When we were all sitting down enjoying our meal, I got Ronald's attention and nonchalantly nodded my head towards Nathan and mouthed the word "now?" He nodded his approval.

"Hey, Nathan, want to hear some exciting news?" I said with a big smile on my face.

"Yeah, what is it," he answered after swallowing a mouth full of mashed potatoes.

"Momma's gonna have a baby."

"Really?" Nathan looked at me, then at Ronald.

"Yes, you're going to be a big brother."

"Wow, that's awesome." Nathan got up from the table and gave me a big hug.

"Is it a boy or girl? When's the baby going to be born?"

"We don't know if it's a boy or girl yet, but the baby should be here sometime in September or October."

"Cool, I'm going to be a big brother."

We finished our dinner, and the three of us snuggled together on the couch to watch TV for the rest of the evening. The following Wednesday, Ronald and I told Ty. He seemed even more excited than Robert. My heart was happy—everyone was excited about the arrival of a new family member. My hopes and dreams were short-lived.

The day had finally come after a couple of weeks of planning Robert's eighth birthday party. I was busy getting the house ready when I started cramping. I thought it was unusual, but I was so busy I didn't have time to give it much thought. I had a house full of boys who were playing and being typical nine-year-olds when the cramping intensified. I mentioned it to Ronald, but he didn't act too concerned. The pain got so bad, I went to the bathroom. To my shock and horror, I miscarried the baby in the toilet.

"Ronald, come here quick," I yelled from the bathroom.

He knocked on the door and I let him in. Crying, I told him what happened.

"Call your doctor and see what we need to do."

I went to my room to make the call as Ronald went to be with the boys enjoying the birthday party. I was in shock and dazed when I told my doctor what had happened. She asked me to bring in the remains the next day and said to get some bed rest. We didn't tell Robert and Ty until after the party was over. I was devastated. Not only did I miscarry a baby I tried so hard to conceive, my hopes and dreams for being a mother again were dashed. Another pregnancy loss trauma to endure.

Even though I was grieving the loss of this baby, I wanted to continue trying. The next month, I had some queasy feelings in my stomach, which could've been a symptom of my body recuperating from the miscarriage. I felt in my spirit I was pregnant again. In my heart, I was certain I was pregnant again.

"I am making an appointment with my doctor," I told Ronald.

"Why? Something wrong?"

"No, I just think I'm pregnant again. I want to have a pregnancy test done at the doctor's office. Because it was only about a month since I had the miscarriage, it seems impossible I could be pregnant again, but I need to settle my mind." I thought I could get a more accurate test at the clinic.

I saw my doctor in the hallway when I was being escorted in the back to have the test. "What are you doing here, Molly?" she asked as I walked by her.

"I'm taking a pregnancy test."

She looked at me as if I were crazy. "I doubt you're pregnant. You just had a miscarriage. Your body needs to recover."

"Well, I need to do this to settle my mind," I responded as I continued to follow the nurse down the hallway.

"Okay. As you wish," she said back to me.

I kicked my legs back and forth as I sat on the examining table waiting for Dr. Morgan to come into the room with the results of my test. I liked Dr. Morgan. She was the first woman doctor I'd ever had. I figured since I had such dreadful experiences with male doctors, I was switching to a woman this time. The door opened, and Dr. Morgan walked in. She had a strange look on her face. I couldn't read her at all. She walked towards me. "I don't know how to explain this. I wouldn't have believed it if I hadn't seen it with my own eyes. You're pregnant."

"Praise the Lord! I knew it. I just knew it," I beamed with excitement trying not to show an I-told-you-so attitude.

"Well, you're right." Dr. Morgan did a brief exam, and we talked about when my due date would be. We figured a November due date.

I couldn't wait to break the news to Ronald and the boys. Nathan and Ty talked about being big brothers.

"I hope it's a boy," Nathan would say to Ty.

"Me, too. We could teach him how to play sports and fish and stuff," Ty answered.

"What if I have a girl?" I said as I jumped into their conversation.

"That'd be okay, I guess," Nathan replied.

"Yeah, I guess," added Ty.

We were all happy, and we prayed daily for the Lord to bless my pregnancy and the baby I was carrying. Everything should be good, right? Not so.

"Hello!" I couldn't tell if the sound of Ronald's voice on the other end of the phone was one of concern or aggravation. This was the second time I'd called him on the job this week, and it wasn't even Friday yet. He could hear me crying on the other end. "What's wrong?"

"I need you to come home," I blubbered.

"What's the matter with you?"

"I don't know what's the matter with me. I just need you to come home." I mumbled out the words between sobs.

"Honey, I can't keep leaving the job site every time you start crying." I could tell Ronald was trying to sound tender, but that was not what I needed to hear. I thought I was losing my mind, and I needed my husband. "It's not that I don't love you or care. It's just this is becoming a regular event. I came home three times last week, and this is the second time you've called me since Monday."

Unlike my other pregnancies, I was overwhelmed with tears and sadness. I couldn't understand why I was feeling such despair, deep remorse, and grief. I was thrilled to be pregnant with my husband's baby. I always wanted more children, but it seemed I'd start crying at the drop of a hat.

In the beginning, I blamed it on hormones. I just knew I was carrying a little girl and thought I was overly emotional with double the female hormones flowing through me. When the tears turned to sobbing, I started getting concerned. I became alarmed when I cried so hard, I needed Ronald there to comfort me no matter what time of day it was.

"What's the matter, Molly? Why are you crying so much?" Ronald said as he came in the door and pulled me close.

"I don't know. I am supposed to be happy. I've wanted this baby for a long time. Why aren't I happy? There's got to be something wrong with me," I said as I buried my face in his shoulder soaking his shirt with tears. Ronald tried his best to comfort me even though he was just as clueless as I was about all the tears. "You're pregnant. All women cry more easily when they're pregnant." He patted me on the back as I sobbed.

I don't cry a lot. I cried for a short time after when I lost the babies, then I was told it was enough. I had to suppress my grief. Something I was used to. When I couldn't control my tears, I thought there was something wrong with me.

"I'm sorry for making you come home again. I just don't know what to do. I don't know what's wrong with me."

"You'll be okay. Call a friend and go shopping for baby stuff. Maybe that'll take your mind off things." Now, when Ronald encourages me to go shopping, I know he's really grasping for something to make me happy. Spending money is not on his list of priorities.

"Do you think I'm going crazy?" I pulled back looking into his eyes to see if there was any sign he thought I was.

His brown eyes were soft and tender as he looked down at me. "No, you're not going crazy. Everything will be all right." I realized it's a man's nature to want to fix things for his wife when she's upset. A woman's tears trigger something deep within a man. Tears bring out a gentleness normally hidden behind a wall of strength. I'm sure a woman's tears may often make a man feel helpless because he can't fix the problem. Normally, all we women want from our men is for them to listen and try to understand how we're feeling.

"Go on back to work. I'll be okay." I wasn't sure at all if I was going to be ok, but I could tell Ronald felt as helpless as I felt, confused by the raw emotion I couldn't control. My eyes were red and swollen. I hated for Ronald to see me like this. I kissed Ronald and pushed him towards the door. He gave me a quick hug and walked out the screen door. He glanced back at me before getting into his truck. I forced a smiled back at him. Get a hold of yourself. You can't keep calling Ronald to come home every time you start crying. You can't have the boys seeing you as an emotional wreck when you are pregnant with their sister. You want this baby desperately; now put on your big girl panties and be happy. I tried to snap out of my sadness by giving myself a good talking to. It worked. Temporarily.

As the months went by and I grew bigger with this baby, my sleep became more restless. Many times, I would wake up during the middle of the night because of horrid nightmares. In one nightmare, I was looking down into a landfill from far above. Everywhere I looked there were mountains of waste. Something about these ominous peaks looked odd. I peered to get a better look at what they were comprised of. To my shock and disbelief, I realized all of them were piles of the remains of human baby bodies. Some were dismembered; some of the bodies were intact. The tormented looks on their decaying faces were shocking. The scene was horrible.

Overwhelmed with feelings of disgust, I became nauseated and repulsed by the sight. A group of people appeared between the mountains of decomposing babies. They acted like archeologists. I could see the repulse, dismay, and disbelief on their faces. I overheard them say, "What's this? What kind of society would kill their children and dump their remains in landfills?"

I knew they had stumbled on the most barbaric civilization they'd ever discovered in the history of humanity. I felt ashamed. The sight of the mutilated bodies traumatized me. I woke breathing heavily, my heart pounding. I was afraid to close my eyes again for fear of seeing the disgusting scene again.

Why would a pregnant woman dream such horrible things? Pregnant women are supposed to be dreaming of the hopes and plans they have for their child. I never spoke of these dreams to anyone. They were too disgusting to even remember, and I thought people would think I was slipping into insanity

The dreams continued causing me to drift deeper into despair. All the while I tried to fight back and be happy with this pregnancy. No one knew the emotional turmoil I was in. I certainly didn't know the root cause.

My beautiful daughter was born in the early evening on November 3. I caught a glimpse of her as they whisked her to the warming bed to check her vitals. She looked purple, greyish purple. I thought it was odd. I kept my eyes on her as the nurses checked her out. Then I heard her start to cry.

"Don't cry, LaRue. Mommy and Daddy are here." I'd been calling my baby girl by her name for months. As soon as she heard my voice, she stopped crying and turned her head towards me. Finally, they brought her to me. LaRue was gorgeous even though her temples started to bruise from the forceps, and there were a lot of little holes in her scalp where the fetal monitor prongs were placed in utero. I fell instantly in love with my little girl. This time there was no birth trauma.

LaRue was the missing link to our family. She completed us. We all loved taking care of her, playing with her, and watching her as she went through her growing stages. Rocking and singing to her was a delight. Once while rocking her, I gazed at her, stroking her head, and admiring her sweet, little face. Without warning or cause, an overwhelming feeling came over me. If anyone ever hurts you, I'll kill them with my bare hands. Wow, where did that come from? The feelings with the thought shocked and scared me. I could actually see myself physically attacking someone for hurting my baby girl. Who thinks of such things? It's not normal? Is it? I put that thought aside and contributed them as a maternal, protective instinct.

My parenting behaviors with LaRue were different from those with Nathan. I became very protective of her. I don't think I was overbearing. Just very watchful trying to prevent her from hurting herself. I adored her and couldn't bear to be away from her for long. Before she came into our lives, Ronald and I would often take overnight weekends away from the boys. Always when Ty was with his mother. Sometime after LaRue was born, we tried an overnight, but it wasn't fun for me. I needed to hurry back home to her. We only did that once. From then on, all the kids went with us if we went anywhere for the weekend.

LaRue was just a few months old when a dramatic event happened that changed the course of my life forever. It all started with a phone call.

I have great sorrow and unceasing anguish in my heart. (Romans 9:2 NIV)

CHAPTER 8

The Painful Truth

The phone rang several times before I could answer. Trying not to sound like I was out of breath, I picked up the receiver, "Hello."

"Hey, Molly, this is Jill. Have you heard Mrs. James Dobson is speaking at the Temple Crisis Pregnancy Center banquet?"

Jill knew I was a big fan of Dr. James Dobson and the Focus on the Family ministry. "That's awesome, Jill. I'd love to go. When is it?"

"The banquet is in February. Dave and I have tickets, but they're sold out. I thought you could call and get on a waiting list."

Of course, I was disappointed, but I wanted to make sure I had a chance to go if there was a cancellation. "I'll call right now and get on the list. Do you have the number?" As soon as I got off the phone, my fingers were dialing the number to Temple Crisis Pregnancy Center. I got on their waiting list. All I could do was pray and trust the Lord would open the door for me to go. A few days before the banquet I got a phone call.

"Hello, is this Mrs. White?"

"Yes."

"This is Carol from Temple Crisis Pregnancy Center. We have one open seat for the banquet tomorrow night. I know this is last minute. Are you still interested in attending?

"Yes, I am."

"Wonderful. You'll be sitting at the Scott and White Memorial Hospital table in Representative Diane White Delisi's seat. She's already paid for the ticket and is donating the seat to whoever takes her place."

Scott and White Memorial Hospital is one of the largest hospitals in Texas. It's also a teaching hospital. The building sits on the highest point in our county and can be seen from miles away.

"That's awesome. I'm looking forward to it." Oh my gosh, I can't believe it. Thank you, Lord, for providing a way for me to attend the banquet. What am I going to wear? I won't know a soul at this table. I've got to go shopping to find something suitable to wear. As soon as I hung up the phone, I called Jill and told her. Then I loaded LaRue in the car and headed to the mall. The banquet was just a few days away. I had no time to spare. I'd never attended a banquet before, so I was a little anxious.

"Hello, my name is Molly White. I'll be sitting in Representative Delisi's seat this evening." My heart pounded as I introduced myself to the strangers sitting at the table.

"Mrs. White, I'm Dr. Raleigh White. A tall, grey-haired man rose from his seat and shook my hand. "This is my wife …" his voice began to fade as he began introducing the other guests seated at the table, and I realized I was sitting with the bigwigs of our community. Doctors, lawyers, CEO's. Dr. White pulled out my chair and helped me sit down as we joked about possibly being related.

"So, Mrs. White, is your husband related to any of Whites from Scott and White?" one of the guests asked.

"Oh, no," I laughed, "his family are farmers, not doctors." I engaged in small talk with everyone as we ate dinner.

"Ladies and gentlemen, welcome to the Annual Temple Crisis Pregnancy Center fundraising banquet. Thank you all for coming tonight." The master of ceremony's voice diverted our attention. I turned my chair, so I could have a better view of the stage.

"I regret to inform you Mrs. Dobson had to cancel her trip to be with us this evening."

I could hear a soft murmur of disappointment flow through the room. Or was that my sigh of disappointment echoing across the room?

"Focus on the Family has sent us a wonderful speaker who, I believe, will touch our hearts and lives in a powerful way. She is Focus on the Family's manager of pregnancy center outreach. Please help me welcome, Sydna Massé."

After a few minutes giving accolades to Mrs. Dobson, James Dobson, and sharing about her work at Focus on the Family, Sydna began to tell us about her life. She grew up as a Catholic and become pregnant in her teen years while working on a degree at a Christian college. Her story took a traumatic twist when she described her decision to abort her baby, and her experiences during and after the abortion.

Her story gripped my heart and was the first time I'd heard anyone talk about their abortion. I guess I thought I was the only one who harbored this secret. Too ashamed to tell anyone. With every descriptive word she spoke, a well of emotion started to stir deep within me. Here I was sitting at a table with strangers—doctors and lawyers on top of that—and having to fight back an eruption of tears and grief that wanted to burst from my aching heart. Her story was my story. Not in the details leading up to her abortion, but in the process and aftermath. Her words were touching on every trigger point I didn't even know existed. I couldn't wait to leave.

When the event was over, I quickly expressed my appreciation to Dr. White and the guests at the table and headed straight for the door. I barely made it to my car when the tears burst through the wall I had erected years ago. I sat in my car and cried so hard I almost hyperventilated. After several minutes, I was able to compose myself enough to be able to drive home. When I got home the kids were already in bed, and Ronald was sitting on the couch watching TV.

"What's wrong? I thought you went to a banquet."

Ronald was surprised to see his wife come in with red puffy eyes. I plopped down on the couch next to him and rested my head on his shoulder.

"A woman shared her testimony about having an abortion as a teenager and how it impacted her life. I've never heard anyone talk about her abortion before. Everything she said I could relate to. It took all the energy I had to hold back my tears and emotions while she was talking. I was sitting with strangers and didn't want them to see me break down because they would know I had had an abortion too. I left as soon as it was over."

The rest of the evening a strange feeling was stirring within me. I need to do something to help pregnant women not make the same mistakes I did. If women and girls heard my story about what happens after abortion, they would certainly choose life for their babies. That's it. I'm going to the Temple Crisis Pregnancy Center and see if I can volunteer.

The next day I picked up the phone and started dialing. My heart started to pound; my hands began to sweat. With every ring of the phone, I became more anxious. Will these women accept me knowing what I did? They work to save lives and mothers, I had two abortions.

"Temple Crisis Pregnancy Center. Can I help you?"

"Yes, my name is Molly White. I attended the banquet last night. I'm interested in volunteering at the center."

"That's wonderful. Please hold and I'll connect you to the director, Kathy," said a woman on the other end.

Kathy and I spoke for some time. We set an appointment for later in the week for an interview. When I arrived at the center for the interview, I was very impressed by the décor and peaceful, homey atmosphere. A volunteer greeted me. She was kind and friendly, pretty close to my age, mid-to-late-thirties. She led me back to Kathy's office chatting the whole time about how she liked volunteering at the center.

"Kathy, Molly White's here."

"Welcome, Mrs. White. Please come in and have a seat."

Kathy appeared to be about ten years older than me. She had slightly greying, medium-length hair and was dressed in slacks and blouse. Her office was warm and welcoming. Pictures of cute babies and mothers and their children lined the walls. A burning candle made the room smell like fresh roses. We sat down and began getting to know each other.

During my interview, I realized I really liked Kathy and what the center offered pregnant women. I didn't know places like this existed. The more she described the services and programs they offered, the more I wished I had known about them when I was pregnant. Within a couple of days, I was volunteering. Day one was spent going through training. I was placed under supervision of other volunteers to help me until I felt comfortable taking clients and calls on my own.

On my first day, Kathy and I were chatting during a break time. During our conversation I mentioned I had had an abortion. I was too ashamed to tell her I had two abortions. I looked closely at her to see if I could see any negative reactions to my confession. Kathy seemed unfazed. She offered her condolences, which I thought was kind but weird. Then, without blinking an eye, she said, "We're offering an abortion recovery program soon. This is the first time our center has offered a program like this. It's called Healing the Hurts of Abortion. It's a fifteen-week Bible study. The group meets once a week, it's free, and totally confidential. Would you be interested in joining us?"

I was aghast. I let out a grunt and rolled my eyes. Abortion recovery? What's that? Is it for crazy, weak-minded women? Does she think I'm weird or an emotional mess?

I leaned towards her with a little self-righteous indignation and full confidence to make myself perfectly clear in my response, "No. I don't need to go through abortion recovery, I've been forgiven. I don't have a problem with my abortion."

Denial. Kathy looked a little shocked, but she never skipped a beat.

"Oh, ok. I thought I'd mention it to you. We have quite a few women already signed up. I thought you'd be interested."

"Thank you, Kathy, but I'm fine."

On my way home, I was consumed with thoughts about the Bible study. I'd attended a lot of Bible studies since I was saved and loved every one of them. Now I was feeling compelled to attend this study, and it was driving me crazy. I couldn't understand why I felt like I needed to go. After all, I didn't have a problem with my abortions. Being ashamed to mention more than one abortion to Kathy should've been a clue I had issues. Denying abortion had any negative effects on me was another big clue. Here I am again, in turmoil. Like the day I was facing an abortion decision, my heart and mind were in conflict. My mind could not conceive why I felt like taking this Bible study. My heart was compelling me to go.

I didn't go to the first meeting. When I returned to the center to volunteer, Kathy stopped by my desk to talk to me.

"Last night was the first night of the Healing the Hurts of Abortion Bible study."

"Yeah, I know."

"I hear they had a good turnout. Six ladies attended."

"That's good."

"It was just an introductory meeting. It's not too late to sign up if you'd like to go."

I rolled my eyes and looked at Kathy, "Nope, I'm fine. Really."

Kathy looked at me with kind eyes, "Ok. I've got some things to do. I'll talk to you later."

We both returned to our duties. Something was happening to me, though. I couldn't figure out what. All I knew was feeling like I had to attend the next meeting. The Holy Spirit was doing something within me, wooing me, compelling me, tugging at my heart. I felt like the Holy Spirit was pushing me. Now I felt a strong desire to go to the Bible study. I could hardly wait until the next meeting.

What's wrong with you? Why do you feel you need to attend this abortion recovery program? You don't have a problem with your abortions. You've been forgiven, remember? My mind was going nuts trying to figure out why the change. I didn't feel the need to go. I felt compelled to go. My heart pondered my predicament. Oh, I know. I feel the need to go to this group so I can learn how to help some poor wretch who has a problem with her abortion. That's it. That's why I'm volunteering at the center, to help women not have an abortion. Now I need to go to this abortion recovery group to help women who have problems after their abortion. I get it, now. That was it. I finally figured out why I needed to attend this study. I was happy with the reason and looked forward to the next meeting.

By time the next Healing the Hurts of Abortion meeting came around, there was no stopping me from attending. Even though I knew the reason why I was going, during the drive to the meeting location I became more and more apprehensive. I arrived early to meet with the group facilitators prior to the other ladies arriving. I didn't know whether to knock on the door or walk on in. As I reached for the handle, the door opened, and an attractive brunette about my age gave me a big smile.

"Hi, Molly, we've been expecting you. We're so happy you are joining us. Cheryl is waiting for you in the other room. She's going to go over some paper work, give you your study book, and brief you on last week's meeting. Debbie escorted me down the hall to a room where Cheryl was sitting at a desk. She opened the door and motioned for me to enter.

"You must be Molly," Cheryl said as she got up to shake my hand.

"Yes, that's me." My voice must have cracked a bit when I responded.

"Don't be nervous. We're in a safe, private place. Have a seat and fill out these forms."

I filled out the information they required and was given the materials needed for the program. Cheryl filled me in on what transpired the week before. As we were talking, I could hear ladies start to arrive. My heart pounded with anxiety. My hands and feet started to sweat. A shadow of shame started to overcome me. I felt like I couldn't face these women.

"Ok, we're done. The ladies are here. Let's go out and meet them.""I'll be there in a minute. Where's the bathroom?" My heart began pounding with feelings of dread of having to face the mystery women in the other room. I felt like I'd been branded with a scarlet "A" and was a part of the dregs of society. In my mind, good and decent women did not have abortions. I had to try and calm my nerves before I showed my face to the rest of the group.

"It's down the hall to the right." Cheryl walked out the door. I could hear the women chatting and laughing as I made my way to the bathroom trying not to be noticed.

I pushed the door opened and locked it behind me. I leaned against the door consumed with shame. How can I face these women? I felt vile. I felt like the worse possible human being, and I was about to be in the company of the same kind. A knock on the door snapped me out of my panic.

"Molly, we're ready to start our meeting. Are you okay?"

"Yes, I'll be right out." I did some deep breaths, trying to calm my racing heart and slowly opened the door. Keeping my head down, looking at the floor, I walked down the hall and into the meeting room. I peeked through my tilted eyes and spotted an empty chair. I slumped into it, looking at the floor the whole time.

"Good evening, everyone. I'm happy to see you all here tonight. We have a new lady joining us tonight, so before we get started, I'd like everyone to introduce yourselves and tell us a little about yourself." Debbie didn't waste any time drawing attention to me.

As I heard the voices of each lady around the room introducing herself, I realized these women weren't tramps like I had imagined. Yes, I thought women who had abortions must be tramps or prostitutes. I counted myself as one of them. These women were normal, everyday women. I raised my head just enough to be able to see around the room and the women sitting around me. They look like me. She's a school teacher? She's a preacher's wife? She's a realtor? She's a recovering addict and lives in a halfway house? She owns a small business? She's a Sunday school teacher? By time the introductions reached me, my head was up, but I couldn't make eye contact.

"My name is Molly White. I'm a stay-at-home mom. I have two sons who are ten years old—one is my stepson—and a baby girl just a few months old."

Cheryl took over from there. The ladies discussed their first week's assignment from the study. This lesson drove home who

God is. Debbie and Cheryl took turns talking about salvation, grace, and God's unfailing love. The whole chapter for this lesson was written to reaffirm that God loves us unconditionally and has great mercy and compassion for us. As the evening progressed, my heart started to calm down and my anxiety subsided. We had a fifteen-minute break, which helped me get to know a couple of ladies a little more. Diane, a preschool teacher and I clicked. She and I had a lot of common interests. I knew we could easily become friends. We returned to the group as the meeting wound down.

"Ladies, work on chapter two. Be prepared to share your testimony with us when we meet again."

Oh, my god. Testimony? You mean I have to tell these women what I did? I have to say it out loud? My heart pounded, my legs prepared for flight as I wanted to get up and run out the door, my stomach muscles squeezed tight like a vice was gripping my mid-section, my chest felt crushed. I could hardly breathe. I left in a hurry, hoping and praying that next week's meeting would be cancelled. It wasn't.

> So Jesus was saying to those Jews who had believed Him, "If you continue in My word, then you are truly disciples of Mine; and you will know the truth, and the truth will make you free. (John 8:31–32 NASB)

CHAPTER 9

THE DAM BREAKS

That week, when Ronald was at work, the boys at school, and LaRue was down for a nap, I sat down to write my testimony. In the quietness of my room, years of anguish, regret, and grief poured onto the paper. As I wrote, things I'd forgotten came to my memory. Buried feelings bubbled to the surface. Tears threatened to burst through the wall I'd built around my emotions. I was physically and emotionally exhausted when I finished.

By time I arrived at the group, I was sick to my stomach. Waves of fear flowed over me as I thought about telling the others what I did. My emotions were tossing me back and forth like being on a ship in the middle of the sea during a raging storm. My stomach gurgled with nausea. I took a seat in a winged-back chair in the living area of our meeting place. All the ladies in my group sat in a semicircle around our leaders. Debbie and Cheryl didn't waste any time. They started our session off with prayer and got right to the testimonies. Participation was on a volunteer system.

"Who wants to go first?"

It sure isn't going to be me. Dread of having to talk about my abortions out loud caused my stomach to churn. I fought to keep the sickness at bay. My heart pounded like the drums of a frenzied rock-n-roll performance. My airways constricted, like a boa snake squeezing his victim of prey, making breathing difficult.

"I'll go."

I looked at Karen, a pastor's wife. I can't believe she volunteered so quickly. She's the bravest woman I've ever seen. Her testimony was heartbreaking. Then Gillian, the young wife; then Carol, the realtor; then Diane, the school teacher; then Shawnda, the recovering addict. Her story was horrifying. Her father and brothers dragged her into an abortion clinic, forcing her to have an abortion.

One by one each woman shared her gut-wrenching story. Tears flowed, sobs and sniffles filled the room. I could relate to certain parts of every woman's story. But it didn't make it any easier on me. My time was approaching quickly. Then all the red and puffy eyes were on me. Everyone had shared. I was the only one left. I could hear a faint rattling of paper. I looked down and realized the noise was caused by the paper in my trembling hands. I could feel vomit rising into my throat. I hate to vomit and was able to keep it down. Breathe. In and out. You can do this. Pretty soon it will be over.

"I had t-t-two abortions." There it was. The first time I'd ever said those words out loud. Tears welled up in my eyes, my throat was raw and aching from suppressing tears. I cried the entire time I read through my story. I didn't know at the time, but I was purging the vileness of guilt, grief, and shame buried deep within my soul for the previous fifteen years. I lost all control of my anguish and pain. As tears streamed down my face, I relived my abortion experiences. Crying turned to sobbing when I told them about my parents pressuring me to have my second abortion.

I made it through my story. I was exhausted, yet relieved. I was no longer sick to my stomach. Besides, even with the sighing and runny, stuffy nose that comes after a good cry, I could breathe better. My heart wasn't pounding. My chest wasn't tight. Everyone showed great compassion towards me, like we did to each other. Then, Deb asked me a weird question.

"Molly, are you still angry at your parents?"

Angry at my parents? I was puzzled by the question.

"No, I'm not angry with them."

"Oh. It just sounded like it when you were sharing your story."

"No, I'm not." I couldn't believe Deb would ask me such a question. I was rather incensed at the idea I would be angry with my parents.

The hardest night was over. Spiritually, I felt like I was on the floor all evening lying in a fetal position, sucking my thumb, and overcome with grief. The crown of denial slipped off my head. The hardest part of coming out of denial is the first tilt of the crown slipping off our head. Our first instinct is to try and catch it before it falls and place it securely back on the center of our head, so we can balance it through life. That's not good when it comes to healing from a traumatic experience. Some of us don't want to deal with the past or guilt for various reasons. It's a choice to live in bondage. I lived in bondage for a decade and a half because I didn't think I could handle the pain I'd buried and didn't know there was a God bigger than my shame and guilt and all-powerful to handle it.

Getting your guilt and pain out in the open is the first step to recovery. When I regurgitated my story and the emotions associated with those memories gushed out, I felt a sense of relief. My abortions and the trauma that ensued were hidden in darkness and were now out in the open. Satan lost his grip, and the Holy Spirit began the healing process.

That night, when my husband and I were in bed, I felt I needed to tell him my story. I only told him I'd had the abortions before we got married. I never told him the details. I wept when I shared what I'd gone through and sobbed when

I told him I was pressured by my parents to have my second abortion. I was in deep travail. The well containing years of unresolved grief overflowed. Tears gushed out like a breeched dam. I grieved. My husband never said a word. He never tried to comfort me. I'm pouring out my soul, and I felt like I was talking to a wall.

The next eleven weeks of abortion recovery were difficult. I had to tread through the sessions alone, without any emotional support from home. My parents found out I was going to this group and tried to dissuade me from participating in the program. They couldn't believe I'd dredge up the past. I was committed, led by the Holy Spirit, to finish.

The following weeks, we dealt with our shame, our guilt, our regret. We learned about God's grace, forgiveness, and redemption. We bonded as women who've experienced the same traumatic experience. We gave our children an identity and named them. Naming my babies took a lot of thought. Family names are really important to me, so I named my first child Willy, after a great uncle on my dad's side, and my third child Ruby, after a great aunt on my mom's side.

Then came the time to prepare for a memorial. We were actually going to have a service like a funeral. I thought it was crazy. I didn't want to go through with it. How can you have a memorial service for someone you've never met? Someone you didn't know? Someone you've never seen? I had a hard time accepting this as part of our recovery process. I did go through with it, reluctantly.

We had a wonderful service. Family members attended. Not mine. Friends attended. One friend attended for me. A pastor led the service, and we, the mothers of aborted children, grieved. The memorial service was closure to a death.

Our last meeting consisted of a celebration. We celebrated life. We celebrated that our children were in heaven, and we'd be reunited one day. It was hard for all of us to say goodbye. We'd shared a lot together, we grieved together, we laughed together, and we bonded through the commonness of our experiences. I'm still in contact with some of the women in my abortion recovery group.

I was stronger by the end of the fifteen-week study. I felt a tremendous release from the burden of unresolved grief. I talked about spilling out the toxic emotions, which ate away at my conscience. I was able to talk to my husband about his strange reaction, or I should say, non-action the night I blurted out the painful details of my abortions and his lack of sympathy and support.

"Honey, I need to ask you something." I snuggled close to my husband as we were lying in bed.

"Yeah? What is it?"

"Why weren't you there for me when I told you about my abortions? Why didn't you support me, or at least try and comfort me during these past weeks? I was hurting. The deepest pain I've ever felt. You said nothing. You did nothing." Tears started to well up in my eyes as my voice cracked with emotion.

After a long period of silence, his voice broke through the darkness.

"I thought you were going to leave me. I didn't know what to do."

"Leave you? I needed you. I had no one to comfort me. No one to reassure me everything would be all right. I suffered through this alone, I had no one to confide in, and you laid next to me every night."

I couldn't believe it. For some reason, my husband thought in all my turmoil, I'd run. Run away from him and my troubles. I have no idea what made him think that, but that's how he felt. He was paralyzed with the fear I would abandon him, and

I was alone in my recovery. We came through the experience a little torn and haggard, but we survived. I had to teach my husband how to comfort me when I needed it. He learned, but I must ask him, or tell him what it is I need, like I need a hug, I need to be held. He's very good at delivering, but not good at picking up clues.

Healing from my abortions took a long time—years. My recovery process took three critical steps. Each step took its own time. Every step included the act of forgiveness.

> For His anger is but for a moment, His favor is for a lifetime; Weeping may last for the night, But a shout of joy comes in the morning. (Psalm 30:5 NASB)

CHAPTER 10

DIGGING DEEPER

During the ten years following my abortion recovery, I focused on raising my family, volunteering at the pregnancy center, and being involved in the women's ministry at my church. But I continued to struggle with depression, anger, and anxiety. When I first experienced bouts of depression, I blamed them on the weather. I seemed to get depressed during grey, cloudy days, which occurred more often during the fall months. Then I became more aware I'd get depressed during the Christmas holidays and Valentine's Day.

I had learned through my recovery group, depression can occur during the anniversary month of our abortion and the baby's birth month. That was the most bizarre thing I'd ever heard. I never calculated or thought about when my babies should've been born. When I did, Willie should've been born in November. I could not recall the due date for Ruby. I had no idea. No clue. The second abortion was so traumatic I'd completely shut down emotionally and buried all memories of it in order to live, to function even though I was very dysfunctional. All I could remember was I had two abortions. In order to be able to calculate Ruby's due date, I had to call my obstetrician and ask her to look in my medical records for the date. I called her office and left a message for her to return my call as soon as she was available. Later in the day, my phone rang.

"Hello, Molly, this is Dr. Graham. My nurse said you needed to talk to me. What's going on?"

"Thank you, for returning my call, Dr. Graham. I'm going through an abortion recovery program. We're planning a memorial for the babies we lost through abortion. I have absolutely no idea when I had my second abortion. Can you look in my medical records, and see if you can find the date when I had the abortion?"

"I'm happy programs are available for women. I'll have my nurse pull your records and get back to you."

"Thank you, I look forward to her call. Thanks, again, Dr. Graham. Have a nice day."

Later that afternoon I got another phone call from the doctor's office.

"Hello, Molly, this is Nancy, Dr. Grahams nurse. The date you're looking for is February 14, 1985."

"February 14? Are you sure?"

"Yes, I'm afraid so."

I'm sure the nurse could hear the shock and disappointment in my voice. I was stunned.

Valentine's Day, 1985. I had an abortion on Valentine's Day? How could a doctor, much less my parent's go along with having an abortion on a day that represents love? My heart sank. Upon learning the date, I knew why I didn't celebrate or get excited about Valentine's Day anymore—not even when my husband and I were courting. I didn't care to receive cards, gifts, or go out for a special date night.

Even after going through abortion recovery and being able to grieve and mourn the death of my children, I continued to encounter feelings of sadness, despair, and depression. These gloomy feelings became so severe at times, I had difficulty getting out of bed. When I began to miss church on Sundays, a dear friend and confidant convinced me to see a professional

Christian counselor. She recommended someone in our town who'd been helping her. What could it hurt? I can't seem to shake feeling blue all the time. Go see her. Maybe she can help figure out what's going on.

I called the counseling office the following Monday and made an appointment for my first professional counseling session.

I arrived at the 1940s bungalow-style home renovated into a counseling office. The white shutters and trim popped against the dark blue paint. The red begonias in the flower pots on the front and back steps were eye catching. The parking area was in the back giving clients more privacy. I liked that.

As I approached the backdoor entrance, the crackling of the pebbled parking lot under my feet matched the popping of my pounding heart. I was apprehensive about talking with a counselor. Were the images of counseling sessions I'd seen on TV shows and movies accurate? People lying on a couch while the counselor sat in a chair next to you writing down information on their pad. I don't know about this. If you, aren't comfortable and don't like it you don't have to go back. I slowly reached for the doorknob, took a deep breath, and walked in. The reception desk was right inside the door.

"Hello, are you Molly?" The attractive, middle-aged woman looked at me with a smile.

"Yes, it's me. I've driven by this house for years and just love the curbside appeal."

"Please have a seat in the waiting area and fill out this paperwork. You can put it on my desk when you're done."

I walked across the hallway into a seating area, which was once the living room of the bungalow. The smell of a burning vanilla candle instantly made me feel comfortable and relaxed. The area was private, I was alone. The décor of the space was like out of a fashion magazine, decorated in my style of a mix of antiques, farmhouse, and Christian art work and sayings. I completed the intake forms as a client exited a counseling room and was scheduling another appointment. When the client left, I got up and took my paperwork to the receptionist.

"Just in time. Dana is ready for you."

A door down the hallway opened, and a petite, middle-aged lady with short spiked hair walked out and greeted me.

"Come on back, Molly. My name is Dana—it's so good to meet you. Come in and make yourself comfortable."

I shook her hand and walked into her counseling room. Bookshelves filled two walls of the small space. Christian artwork covered the walls. The seating area had a couch, chair, a coffee table with a box of tissues on it, and a bowl of stress balls for squeezing.

A couch, I knew it. I'm not lying on it. I took a seat on the couch and placed my purse on the floor next to me.

Dana sat in a chair across from me, notepad on her lap. "How can I help you, Molly?"

"I don't know. I've been feeling blue, even depressed, for a long time. It's especially bad around this time of year. During the late fall and early winter months, the symptoms are worse. Christmastime is the worse. I try to provide wonderful Christmas memories for my kids, but I'm sad and blue the whole month. I figured it was the gloomy weather during the winter months causing the feelings, but now the symptoms persist throughout the year."

"Have you had any other loss or traumatic event recently?"

"No. I'm not sure what's causing me to feel this way."

I told Dana about my abortions, going through abortion recovery, and how my parents and family reacted when I was going through the recovery program,

"Why did your parents call to try and discourage you from going through the Bible study for healing?"

"I don't know. They weren't happy about it at all." She wrote something on her note pad.

Dana was kind, engaged in the conversation, and understanding. I felt very comfortable talking to her. Then she asked me a question I'd never thought about.

"Are you taking any medications for depression or anxiety?"

"No, I never thought about it. I don't even know anything about them."

Dana explained the differences among the medications and suggested I see a psychiatrist to discuss what I was experiencing and find out if there was a medication that might help me with the symptoms of depression. She gave me several referrals.

The hour went by rather quickly. Time was up. I didn't feel like I was any better off, but certainly not worse off.

"Try to get in to see a psychiatrist before our next appointment. I believe using an antidepressant or an anxiety medication may help you as you continue counseling. I'd like to see you again next week."

"Ok, I'll call one of these doctors and see if I can get in quickly."

We said our goodbyes, and she asked if she could give me a hug. I accepted her offer.

I did get in to see a psychiatrist. Through the next several weeks, I tried several types of treatments before I decided an antianxiety medication worked best for me. I continued my sessions with Dana. Each week our session started out about the same, "How was your week? How are you doing today? What would you like to talk about?" For several weeks, I couldn't even tap into what was going on. I was so shut down, so depressed, I didn't know how I felt about anything.

On more than one occasion, Dana would give me a paper with a list of emotions in two columns to help me identify how I was feeling. I had become so shut down I couldn't articulate or recognize the feelings I was having except anger and sadness. I was shocked when I read through the long list of emotions. I would identify an emotion or feeling and say, "I feel like this, and this, and this." Emotions like anger, fearful, and hopeless.

I talked about my parents often to Dana. It seemed like everything they did irked me and caused me to get angry. After complaining about their behavior one particular session, Dana responded, "Why does the way they act bother you so much?"

"Why does it bother me so much? What do you mean?" I went on and on. "They do this, and they do that …"Dana asked, again, "Why do they bother you so much?"

I snapped back at her, "Why does it always have to be about me? Can't you see their behavior? They do this stuff that irritates me all the time. Why can't they be held responsible? Why does it always have to be about me?"

In her normal, soft and gentle voice she replied, "Because you're the one who's upset about it. You're the one it's bothering."

"Urgh." I growled under my breath. She was right. I was the one upset, and she was trying to get at the root issue, which didn't happen right away.

Dana was like a miner, guiding me through the process of digging through layers of emotions and memories to help me find the center of my being where the root causes of my depression, anxiety, and anger issues were rooted.

The process of digging through each layer continued week after week until I finally reached the core issue. When I first started counseling, I didn't know the first thing about getting to the primary sources of my woundedness. I didn't even know I had core issues much less unresolved grief and trauma.

Dana carefully guided me through the process. She was there for me when I felt like I was suffocating and had to come up for air. The Holy Spirit was there to comfort me, guide me, protect me, and show me what I needed to see, and to haul off the debris of all the unresolved issues and emotions I dealt with along the way. The Spirit tenderly healed each layer, so I could continue my journey.

After many months of digging and healing, the light of the Holy Spirit found the root of my depression, anger, and resentment. During one counseling session, I broke down and wept as I realized I felt rejected and abandoned by my parents. When they pressured me to have my second abortion, I felt they didn't love me or my baby when I needed them the most. I felt shunned and shamed.

After my forty-fifth birthday celebration, while I was reflecting on the evening filled with family and friends, out of the clear blue, the Lord spoke to my spirit and showed me something hidden in my heart.

"You've got a root of bitterness and hatred towards your parents."

"No, I do—" I was shocked and immediately wanted to deny those feelings, but I couldn't. The Lord had just exposed my heart for me to see. I had a hard time admitting I had deep-seated feelings toward my parents, much less feelings of hatred and bitterness. I loved my parents and wanted a close relationship with them. However, my abortion had driven a huge wedge in our relationship—a wedge neither my parents nor I had known was there. But there it was. The light of the Holy Spirit shone brightly on it. I saw all its ugliness and was repulsed by the feelings stirring in the compartments of my own heart.

Looking back, I knew I really hadn't forgiven them, because everything they said or did rubbed on an unhealed wound causing me to react negatively. That doesn't happen when you're reconciled with those who've hurt you. The Holy Spirit prompted me to forgive my parents—in person.

105

And don't sin by letting anger control you. Don't let the sun go down while you are still angry, for anger gives a foothold to the devil. (Ephesians 4:26–27 NLT)

CHAPTER 11

FORGIVE, FORGIVE, FORGIVE

Oh, no, I can't do that, I argued with the Holy Spirit. If I confront my parents, they'll just put all the blame on me and make me feel guilty and shamed. I can't handle going through that. I just can't.

I battled in my mind, thinking of all the reasons not to personally face my parents about those painful memories. After a few moments of resistance, I realized I had to surrender.

"Ok, God, I'm willing to forgive my parents, but you're going to have to make all the arrangements and prepare their hearts to receive what I have to say." I boldly bargained with God. To my surprise, God arranged the meeting the following day.

God, the creative being he is, arranged for my parents to call me the next morning needing help with their computer. I told my mom I'd be over within the hour. I didn't go to their house very often while I was going through counseling. I was too raw and emotionally fragile. I had to separate from the source of a lot of my pain.

"Boy, you don't fool around, do you? Are you afraid I'll chicken out?" I joked with the Lord about his fast timing. "God, you're clever, aren't you?"

I quickly called Ronald.

I had told Ronald about the arrangement and asked him to be on standby. I couldn't face my parents alone to talk about something that hurt me so deeply.

"I need you to be there for me, Ronald. I can't do it without you. When I call you, please get to Mom and Dad's ASAP."

Ronald was very supportive and agreed to meet me at my parents' home—the final encouragement I needed to go through with the meeting.

"Hello."

"Today's the day. Mom and Dad need help with their computer, so I'm getting ready to go over there. Be ready to head there the next time I call you."

"Ok. I'll be praying for you."

I needed to hear that. I quickly got ready and headed to my parents' house. It was only a fifteen-minute drive. I prayed all the way. Little did they know what awaited them after I solved their computer issue. Little did I know how I was going to approach the discussion.

As soon as I solved the technical problems they had, I grabbed my cell phone and gave Ronald his "signal call." His phone rang, and I hung up. I didn't want my parents to be suspicious of anything.

My parents and I sat in their den and engaged in small talk. They still weren't aware of the real reason I was there. My mind was preoccupied with what I was going to say, and how I was going to say it while I was waiting from my husband to show up. My heart pounded as I began to feel anxious.

Ronald arrived in record time. He knocked on the door before walking in. My parents got up to greet him.

"Hey, Ronald, what're you doing here?" My dad reached to grab Ronald's hand with a firm handshake. "Don't have anything going on at work today?"

"Yeah, I'm on a job, but wanted to stop by for a few minutes."

"Hello, Ronald." My mother gave him a hug. "Come in and have a seat."

Mom took her seat on the maroon, leather love seat under a window. She sat with her hands folded on her lap. Dad took his seat in the matching recliner across the sitting area. Ronald and I sat next to each other on the couch. I reached for his hand and held it firmly.

"Mom, Dad, I need to talk to you about something."

Mom looked at Dad and then at me. I could see her frown. Dad looked at me with curiosity.

"Last night, after my birthday party, the Lord showed me I've been harboring a root of unforgiveness, anger, and bitterness toward you because of you pressuring me to have my second abortion." I could feel the tears working their way up from the recesses of my heart. I fought hard keep them from bursting through and making it difficult for me to say what I had to say.

"First of all, I'd like to ask you to forgive me for dishonoring you by being sexually promiscuous when I was younger." Humbling myself and taking responsibility for my rebellious actions as a young woman opened the door for me to be candid with them. I could see my mother's blue eyes soften.

"When you pressured me to have my second abortion, I felt complete abandonment and rejection by you. I felt you didn't love me or my baby. I've never been so hurt." I could feel the toxic feelings in the center of my heart tossing within me as ice cold water of reconciliation was being dumped on them.

"That abortion almost led to my destruction. I was angry, sad, guilt-ridden, and suicidal. I resented you because you weren't there for me when I needed you, and you pressured me to do something I didn't want to do."

I could see tears well up in my mother's aging, light blue eyes. The eyes that were normally sparkling and full of life and happiness turned a deeper blue with sadness. My dad choked up. I saw his bottom lip quiver as he tried to hold back his emotions.

"Molly."

"Let me finish, Mom. I need to finish. You and Dad have five grandchildren in heaven. They're my children. I named the two babies who were aborted. Your oldest grandchild's name is Willie. He'd be about seventeen years old now. My third child's name is Ruby. She'd be about thirteen. I miss them, feel empty and incomplete without them, just like I do with Nathan's brothers and the child I miscarried, who I believe was a little girl. I named her Josie. I deeply regret having aborted two of my innocent babies and never being able to hold them, kiss them, or experience the joy of watching them grow. Every family gathering and holidays are a painful reminder I don't have all my children with me."

A few tears were able to escape the dam I'd built and rolled down my cheeks. I squeezed Ronald's hand. He squeezed back. My throat was raw with the emotions held captive for many years. "I've suffered in silence the whole time because we never talked about it. I came here today, by the leading of the Holy Spirit, to say I forgive you for pressuring me into something I didn't want to do—abort another baby."

There, I did it. The toxic feelings were purged from within me. I felt light and free. Feelings I'd never felt before.

Mom glanced at Dad and looked at me, her hands still folded on her lap. "We accept your forgiveness. When your Dad and I converted to Catholicism, the first thing we confessed was the abortion."

I could hear her voice choke up with tears.

"The priest said we needed to ask you for forgiveness or there would never be reconciliation between us." My dad let out a sob as my mother shared their first confession.

I was stunned. I was so consumed with my own guilt, pain, and suffering it never occurred to me my parents ever had any feelings of sorrow, guilt, and regret. Somehow knowing this and the act of forgiving them caused my heart to have compassion for them. For the first time, I saw them as human beings who make mistakes, like me.

Forgiving my parents liberated me from years of anger, resentment, bitterness, and hatred. I felt as if I'd been dragging my parents and all the ugly feelings I had around with me like a huge, iron ball chained to my ankle. Once the chain was broken, through the act of forgiveness, I was free from the shackles and heavy burden.

I left their house that day feeling like I was a thousand pounds lighter. I was walking on clouds. My spirit soared like a snared bird released from captivity. I had no idea how much bondage I was in until the Holy Spirit led me to freedom. I never knew those toxic feelings were within me. With guidance and encouragement from my counselor, I was able to allow the Holy Spirit to guide, protect, and heal me. God took the toxic emotions and turned them into love, peace, mercy, and compassion. On my drive home, I felt so liberated and free. All I could do was cry out, "Free at last, free at last, oh, thank God, I'm free at last."

Forgiving my parents allowed me to serve the Lord unhindered by anger. I was no longer bound to my past. I could move forward to defend life with more empathy and resolve. Being forgiven broke the chains of death that ensnared me. Forgiving my parents unleashed me from unhealthy emotional bondage.

I sought and asked Jesus to forgive me. Being forgiven by God liberated me from the burden and punishment of sin and reconciled me with our Father. Forgiving all those who were involved in my abortion decision and with my abortions set me free from the bondage of bitterness, hatred, and anger. I understood the last step was to forgive myself. Forgiving myself didn't mean I was forgiving my sin, rather I recognized what I had done violated me as a woman and caused the death of my children. I recognized I had made a huge mistake, but I needed to come to terms with that and stop punishing myself.

The result of the final step, forgiving myself, was I was able to enter the promised land of freedom. I was free. Free at last. I cried the mantra made famous by the late Martin Luther King Jr. "Free at last, free at last, Thank God almighty, we are free at last." I had no idea how much bondage I was in until I went through those stages.

But God wasn't through with me yet.

"Teacher, which is the greatest commandment in the Law?" Jesus replied: "'Love the Lord your God with all your heart and with all your soul and with all your mind.' This is the first and greatest commandment. And the second is like it: 'Love your neighbor as yourself.' (Matthew 22:36-40 NIV)

Bear with each other and forgive one another if any of you has a grievance against someone. Forgive as the Lord forgave you. (Colossians 3:13 NIV)

CHAPTER 12

HERE I AM, LORD

On the morning of July 24, 2001, years before I had forgiven my parents and myself, I was sitting on my front porch, minding my own business, drinking coffee, and listening to the birds chirping while they were gorging on seeds in a nearby birdfeeder. I began my ritual of reading a Proverb a day during my early morning quiet time.

As I read chapter 24, verses 11-12, it was as if the heavens had opened, the clouds parted, and God's thunderous voice burst through the blue sky like a sonic boom rumbling across the sky, vibrating everything on the ground and in my body, and spoke those verses directly to me, "Rescue those who are being led away to death! Indeed, hold back those who are staggering to the slaughter! If you say, 'Behold, we did not know this,' doesn't he who weighs the hearts consider it? He who keeps your soul, doesn't he know it? Shall he not render to every man according to his work?"

His words fell on me like a crushing weight upon my chest. I gasped for breath as I peeled myself off the back of the rocking chair I felt pinned to. I sat up straight hoping the air would flow better into my lungs. I believe God just called me to do something. I was a bit dazed, but I knew that God had just spoken directly to me.

I had no idea what he wanted me to do, but I had a feeling it had something to do with my abortions. At that time, my dearest friends and I were going through The Sacred Romance

Bible study. I couldn't wait to share my experience with them during our next meeting.

"I've got to tell y'all what happened to me this week." Carrie, Kim, Janie, Gigi, and Brenda gave me their full attention, anxious to hear what I had to say. I recounted my experience on my front porch.

"I think God's calling me to do something, but I have no idea what it could be."

"You think?" said Carrie laughing out loud.

Everyone took turns encouraging me, praying for me, and even prophesying over me. They all knew my abortion testimony and witnessed my healing process After the study, all the ladies left except me. I wanted to stay and talk with Carrie, who hosted the study in her home.

I paced back and forth in her kitchen mumbling and trying to resolve in my mind what God was wanting of me. I blurted out, "What could he be calling me to do? I've pondered over it, prayed about it, fretted over it, and I'm still clueless."

"I'm sure he'll show you in due time. Try not to worry about it." Carrie was calm and patient with my musings.

"I'm not worried, I just want to know what he's trying to say to me. I know it has something to do with my abortions. But what?"

I had no peace. I needed to know what he was asking of me. What did it mean to "rescue those being led away to death?" I'm volunteering at the pregnancy center. I've helped a lot of pregnant women and girls choose life for their babies. That's very rewarding. I've even lost some who were determined to have an abortion. That's painful, but I prayed they'd find you, God, and seek forgiveness and healing.

I felt whatever our Father God was calling me to do was different. Standing in my best friend's kitchen, feeling the anguish and frustration of not knowing what our Lord wanted me to do, I raised my hands in the air, and said, "Here I am, Lord, send me. I'll do what you want me to do, I'll go where you want me to go, and I'll speak what you want me to speak. I surrender to you. Use me, O Lord."

Boy, God didn't waste any time setting me on a course of kingdom work I'd never dreamed of.

Later that week, I was heading to my counseling session when I heard Allan Parker, President of the Justice Foundation, a nonprofit, pro-life law firm based out of San Antonio, Texas, speaking on American Family Radio. Allan and his firm were representing Norma McCorvey, the Roe of Roe vs Wade and Sandra Cano, the Doe of Doe vs Bolton. These two ladies were filing motions seeking to overturn their cases, alleging both cases were based on lies and fraudulent information. The Justice Foundation also represents women who suffer their abortion experience. They were aware of the risks and consequences of legal abortion.

My ears couldn't believe what I was hearing. I was fully tuned in to this interview, absorbing every word, and driving at the same time. Is my mind playing tricks on me? This man is talking about ending abortion and publicly telling how abortion hurts women. I was completely blown away when Allan spoke of a project of his law firm called, Operation Outcry (OO). This project helped women who had been hurt by abortion and wanted to share their stories publicly or through written affidavits.

Allan offered listeners an opportunity to participate in this motion by sharing their personal experiences through legally admissible affidavits. These testimonies would support one of the claims made by the motion: abortion hurts women psychologically, physically, emotionally, and spiritually. My spirit soared. I knew that I had to share my story. Is this it, Lord? I want America to know how abortion hurt me. Women need to know the lifelong consequences of abortion. Lawmakers and judges need to know how legal abortion exploits and hurts women. They need to hear my story.

I was almost to my counselor's office when the host said, "Allan, after the commercial break, I want you to tell women who want to share their stories how they can get in touch with the Justice Foundation. Don't go away, we'll be right back after the commercial break."

Oh, no. Lord, I need to get that contact information. I'm already running late and now I'm in a time crunch. I pressed harder on the gas pedal and careened into the parking lot. I slid into the gravel parking spot leaving a cloud of dust in the air, shoved the gear shift into park, grabbed my purse, and jumped out of my car. Running through the dust cloud I'd just created, I reached the counselor's office door within seconds. My heart was racing, I could barely catch my breath as I raced to the receptionist's desk.

"Quick, turn on AFR radio. Hurry."

The receptionist was confused and spun her chair around looking for the radio. "What's going on? Is there a tragedy somewhere?"

Poor thing. I must've turned her calm morning into instant panic. "No, no. I've got to get the contact information to a place called the Justice Foundation. Hurry. They went to commercial break when I was turning into the parking lot. I need that information."

She found the station just in time. The host was just coming back from commercial break and briefing the listeners on the previous segment.

"Allan, why don't you give the listeners the contact information for the Justice Foundation."

"Ladies, if you've been hurt by abortion and want to share your testimony in support of our motion to overturn Roe vs

Wade based on these facts: Norma never had or wanted an abortion and regrets her involvement in Roe vs Wade. Sandra never gave permission to use her name as a plaintiff in the Doe vs Bolton case and wants the case overturned. Scientific facts prove life begins at conception, abortion takes an innocent human life, and abortion hurts women, you can email the Justice Foundation at ..."

"Quick, I need something to write with." I was scanning her desk for pen and paper, but she was already on top of it. With pen in hand and sticky notes ready, she wrote down the email address, ripped the note from the stack and handed it to me with a smile. I didn't see any condemnation or judgment on her face. Just warm, caring eyes.

"Here you go. Dana is ready to see you now."

I thanked her and went to my counselor's office. I told Dana all about my experiences that week and about hearing Allan on the radio. She agreed with me. We believed God had a plan, and this might be a door he was opening for me.

When I got home, I sat down at my computer and began writing my story to send to the Justice Foundation. I wrote page after page of memories, details, and pain. I choked back tears as painful memories poured out on the pages. Facts came out I hadn't remembered in a long time. The Healer took me a little deeper into the chambers of my heart where I had hidden so much pain. It's one thing to share your story verbally. It's entirely different when you write it.

I finished my story and attached it to an email to the Justice Foundation. In the email, I mentioned a vision I had when I was going through Healing the Hurts of Abortion. I know this vision had to have been from the Lord. I saw a multitude of women gathered together crying and wailing. They were wearing black mourning clothes. I knew in my spirit these women were crying over the loss of their children through abortion. I knew the location had to be Washington, DC. I finished my email, attached my testimony, and clicked the "send" button.

Instantly, my chest began to feel constricted like an anaconda snake was squeezing the breath out of me, my heart could barely beat, my stomach turned to knots. I couldn't breathe or move. I was hit with a full-fledged panic attack. I just poured my guts out to these people I don't even know. I told them about that vision. They're going to think I'm crazy. There's no way I can take it back. God, help me. I calmed myself down enough to call Carrie and tell her everything I had just done. She was unfazed.

"Molly, they're not going to think you're crazy. Obviously, the people at this law firm are Christians. They should know about visions, and as far as your testimony goes, it's your story. How can they judge it?"

The more Carrie spoke, the more she made sense. My chest started to ease, my heart began to beat in its normal pattern, and I could take in a full breath. The panic attack subsided, but my apprehension did not completely leave.

Late that afternoon, I noticed an email from the law firm. I was surprised how quickly I heard back from them. It was a generic note thanking me for my interest and instructing me how to fill out the attached affidavit and get it notarized. I was surprised there was no mention of my vision or my lengthy testimony. I printed the affidavit and sat down to fill it out. I answered the questions with as much detail as space allowed. The following day, I took the affidavit to be notarized by a friend. When I left, I stuffed the form in an envelope I'd prepared to be mailed and dropped it at the post office a few blocks away. There, it's done. Lord, please use my story for your kingdom purposes. In Jesus name, I pray, amen. I felt good about myself. Now, my story could be used to help end legal abortion.

When I got home, I saw another email from the Justice Foundation. This time it was from Allan Parker. Wow, Allan Parker, the man I heard on the radio is contacting me. I was stunned. He thanked me for sharing my testimony and vision with them. He said he, too, had had a similar vision. He noticed I lived just a couple of hours from San Antonio and invited me to come meet them. I accepted. I invited my friend, Kim, ride along with me. We went the following Wednesday—the day they have a prayer meeting during the noon hour.

I got to know the folks at the Justice Foundation (JF) and began forming friendships. Allan called me shortly after our first meeting in early August and told me he'd been invited to attend a pro-life media event in Washington DC. The event was hosted by a well-known pro-life activist named Janet Folger Porter. Janet was kicking off a campaign called Shake the Nation Back to Life. Part of the campaign was to send baby rattles to every member of Congress asking them to support the partial-birth abortion ban. National pro-life and pro-family leaders were going to speak in support of the bill and the campaign. Allan was one of the invitees and speakers.

"Molly, I'd like to ask if you'd be willing to go with me. It's important to have a post-abortive woman representing Operation Outcry (OO) at these events. I can't promise anything, but you may have an opportunity to speak and share your story."

I was shocked he asked me. I immediately accepted the invitation.

"You'll have to cover your own expenses. Is that okay?'

"Yes, can I bring my nine-year-old daughter?"

"Yes, that will be great. By the way, a former law student of mine works for President Bush. He's his scheduler. He's going

119

to try and get us an appointment with the First Lady while we're in DC. Interested in going with me?"

"Of course, what an honor it would be to meet Laura Bush and share my story with her."

My mind barely had the time to process our discussion when I was hit with another panic attack. This time the attack was so bad, I went down to the floor and curled up in a fetal position. I couldn't breathe, I couldn't move. Fear gripped me with the prongs of death. Amid my panic, I heard the voice of the Lord speak softly in my ear. "Who are you afraid of?"

Everyone, Lord. Don't you know they'll stone me if I tell them I had two of my little babies killed? I'll face rejection and condemnation. I'll be hated by the world. Before I could say those words out loud, this is what came out of my mouth, "I fear you, Lord, and you alone. You have said 'Has the blood of my son, Jesus, not washed your sins as white as snow? Do I not remember your sins no more? Don't I hold the keys to heaven and hell? Do I not hold your life in the palms of my hands? What can man do to you?'"

Still lying on the floor, I answered the Lord. "Okay, Lord, I'll go and do what you send me to do." The panic dissipated, I could breathe again, and a sense of calmness fell over me.

So do not fear, for I am with you; do not be dismayed, for I am your God. I will strengthen you and help you; I will uphold you with my righteous right hand. (Isaiah 41:10 NIV)

CHAPTER 13

As I was planning to go to DC, I realized I needed to tell my little girl about my abortions. The thought sickened me, but I knew I had to tell her. I'd already told the boys. They were both quick to forgive me and move on.

When I told LaRue, she listened, put her arms around me, and hugged me. She asked questions and cried a little. I asked for her forgiveness, and she gave it. That night, she told me she'd always wanted a sister closer to her age. Her words stabbed me in the heart.

"You do have sisters and brothers in heaven, LaRue. One day, we'll all be reunited and be one big, happy family." I shared their names with LaRue and prayed with her. She adjusted well in the following days, weeks, months, and years.

On September 3, 2001, with my daughter by my side and a little fear in my heart, we flew with Allan to Washington, DC. During the media event, Janet invited me to share my testimony in response to a reporter's question, "If you take away the supply, what about the demand?"

"I don't think anyone's more qualified to answer that question than Mrs. White." Janet turned from the mic and looked at me. I glanced at Allan, looked at all the leaders standing behind me, and those who were sitting in the audience as I approached the mic. It was surreal. I couldn't believe I was at the National Press Club. Reporters, cameramen, and television crews were everywhere. I spotted my daughter standing on a chair in the back of the room where all the TV cameras were lined up. One of the cameramen was helping her watch me through the lens of the camera. That made me smile and calmed my nerves.

My voice trembled. "I'd like to begin my story by saying I was once pro-choice. You see, I had to be because I had two abortions. If I couldn't defend my decisions to abort two of my children, then I'd have to face the ugly truth: abortion hurts women and kills babies. For thirteen years, I ran from the truth and the memories of my abortions.

"Drugs and alcohol helped me numb the pain. Denial, suppression, and justification helped me cope with the guilt, shame, regret, and deep remorse. Death wooed me to end my life. Then I met a man named Jesus. Have you heard of him? Jesus forgave me and by his blood washed my sins as white as snow. He took my punishment for killing two of my babies by hanging on a cross, so I could be reconciled to the Father. That's why I'm here today, to share my story. Abortion hurts women. Abortion is the problem, not the solution. Pregnant women aren't lining up demanding abortion. Legal abortion exploits pregnant women during their time of need. Pregnant women need love, support, and encouragement to have their babies. Not abortion."

I did it. I was shaken but proud, and relieved it was over. I said what needed to be said in the short time I had. After the event, Janet and other participants thanked me for sharing my story. Their words encouraged me.

That evening, Allan called my room with good news. "Molly, I just got off the phone with Stephen. Mrs. Bush is not available to meet us, but he invited me to meet with him in the West Wing of the White House. Do you and LaRue want to go?"

I almost screamed in his ear. "Of course, we want to go. Are you kidding me? We get to go to the White House?"

"Yes. Bring your written testimony. We'll give him the press packet I prepared for the media event yesterday and your testimony. I'll tell him what we want to relay to Mrs. Bush. I'll need your social security number, driver's license, date of birth, height, weight … for security clearance."

I was up early primping and carefully selecting what I was going to wear. I got LaRue's clothes out and fixed her hair. We met Allan in the lobby and grabbed a muffin before flagging down a taxi and heading to the White House. I could barely contain my excitement. It wasn't long before the three of us stood in a lobby of the West Wing waiting for Stephen to meet us. I looked at everything in every room we passed by and the hallways we walked through. I didn't want to miss anything.

We were escorted into a small waiting area and told by a staffer Stephen would be joining us in a few minutes. Allan and I were both excited and honored to be there, but able to maintain our composure.

"Look, there's the original painting of George Washington crossing the Delaware." I exclaimed with uncontained enthusiasm as I pointed at the hallowed painting.

Another staffer stopped by and let us know Stephen was on his way to meet us.

"What's in that room?" I asked him, pointing to a door joining the waiting area.

"That's the Briefing Room. The President is in there now with members of his Cabinet for a morning briefing. Is there anything I can get you all while you're waiting?"

"No, no, we're fine." I said in almost a daze. President Bush is within a few feet of us behind that closed door. Oh my, goodness. I wonder if he'd mind if I just popped my head in and said a quick 'hello.' After all, we live not too far from his ranch in Crawford. We could start a conversation on that alone. I wanted to knock on that door and pop in, but my thoughts and attention quickly snapped back to reality when I heard a man's voice behind me.

"Allan, it's great to see you. Welcome to the West Wing. Come on back to my office."

Stephen had joined us in the waiting area while I was mesmerized with thoughts of meeting President Bush. Allan introduced me and LaRue as we were following Stephen down a narrow hallway leading to a little nook, which turned out to be his office. Allan told him why we were in DC, filled him in on the motion, and asked me to share a bit of my testimony. We left Stephen all the information we brought. He assured us he'd give it to Mrs. Bush.

I was disappointed we didn't get to meet President or Mrs. Bush, but what an honor just to be in the West Wing of the White House and leave my testimony for Mrs. Bush to read. Allan and I prayed after our meeting. He flew back to Texas that night. LaRue and I stayed another day to do some sightseeing.

On January 21, 2002, LaRue and I flew back to our nation's capital to attend the annual national March for Life. Sharing my testimony publicly spurred me into wanting to do more for the pro-life movement. Attending the march was another turning point for me.

I had a sign that read, "Abortion Hurts Women, Men, and Families" in big white letters on a black background. The subtitle read, "Abortion hurt me, ask me how." A big, red, broken heart was centered on the sign. It was an attention-getter.

The following day, LaRue and I got dressed and headed to the bus stop to catch a ride to the Washington Mall. We sat towards the front where the seats faced the center aisle. We took a seat and I leaned my sign on my legs, front facing me. I nodded and smiled at the elderly black woman sitting directly across me from and LaRue.

"Mom, why are you hiding your sign?"

I looked down at LaRue. She was challenging me to be brave when I was feeling insecure. "You're right, LaRue." I turned my sign around and caught the eyes of the woman. The sign was now facing her. The woman read my sign, looked at me, and nodded in agreement. We talked about abortion and how it was negatively impacting the black community until it was time for LaRue and me to get off. The woman and I said our 'goodbyes' as she wished us a nice day.

After marching for a while, LaRue wanted to stop and rest for a few minutes. We found a tree planter on the sidewalk. I helped her up to sit on the ledge, then pulled myself up beside her. We watched the marchers go by with those on the sidewalks cheering them on. Then I noticed a woman walking towards me. Her eyes were fixed on mine as she got closer and closer to me and my daughter. Oh boy, I wonder what she wants? I started to feel a little apprehensive about a possible confrontation. She walked up to me, pointed at my sign and said, "Does that sign mean you've had an abortion?"

"Yes, it does." I braced myself for her response.

"I had an abortion too."

For the next several minutes, as thousands of pro-lifers walked past us, she shared her story. We bonded over our common experiences. I encouraged her to get involved in an abortion recovery program. As we talked, my eye caught sight of a sign that stood high above the rest in the midst of the march. The sign read, "Pray to keep abortion legal." I caught a glimpse of a woman carrying the sign.

At first glance, I couldn't believe what I'd just read. Then it hit me. There's a pro-choice protestor walking in the midst of the crowd. I sensed in my spirit this woman was trying to justify an abortion decision and was challenging the pro-lifers around her.

125

"Come on, let's catch up to that person. I bet she's had an abortion.

"How do you know?" the young woman asked as I helped LaRue off the tree planter and pushed back into the crowd.

"Excuse us … excuse us," I muttered as we weaved in and around the crowd to catch up with the protestor.

"There she is." The three of us moved up beside her. I could feel a wall of tension around her like a force shield on a spaceship. The middle-aged woman stood straight, her eyes fixed in front of her, and her face hardened with determination.

"Excuse me, can I ask you a question," I said as I walked next to her.

Not even looking at me she barked, "What is it?"

"Are you post-abortive?"

"Post what?"

"Post-abortive?"

"I don't even know what that means."

Someone from the crowd behind us yelled out, "It means have you had an abortion?"

"Yes, yes, I have," she said defiantly and proudly.

That gave me the opportunity to try and relate to her. "LaRue, stay close," I instructed as I stepped in front of the woman and marched backwards so I could talk to her face to face as I told her my story.

"Years ago, I might've been right here marching alongside you because I had to justify my own abortion. The truth is my abortions hurt me deeply. I regret aborting my children and miss the relationships I would've had with them. I'm sorry you've had that experience too. I want you to know no one judges you here. God is a merciful God. If you repent, he will be quick to forgive and begin healing and restoring you. Jesus loves you and so do I."

I took LaRue's hand, turned back around and continued marching. A few seconds later, I looked behind me and the protestor was gone. She had disappeared. I couldn't see her sign or her anywhere. I said a prayer for her asking God to reveal himself to her and to minister to her broken and wounded heart. We finished the march at the Supreme Court and headed back to our hotel.

When I returned from the March for Life, I became the Texas Leader of OO, and actively got involved in helping the JF and their efforts to bring their motion to the Supreme Court. Women were joining us at a fast rate. We held conferences around the country and followed the motion through the circuit court appeals process. I shared my testimony dozens of times and heard hundreds of painful, heartbreaking stories, which made my story pale in comparison.

We immediately embarked on a nationwide campaign to reach women who had been hurt by legal abortion and invited them to join our efforts to end Roe vs Wade. I was on the leadership team, which organized a national media campaign to kick-off the filing of Norma's and Sandra's motions at the Dallas Federal District Court. We felt, because this was the place where Roe vs Wade started, this was the place where it needed to end. I did radio interviews to promote the event and invited post-abortive women to join us. Norma McCorvey was there with Allan to file her motion. She delivered a powerful message during our media event about why she wanted to overturn her case.

About seventy women from across the country met us in Dallas for the motion filing kick-off event. We spent a day and night together at a local hotel getting to know each other and preparing for the event. Every lady was required to share her three-minute written testimony. I split them into two groups in two different rooms. LaRue and I heard dozens of stories.

That night while my ten-year-old daughter and I were lying in bed, LaRue said to me, "Mom, if I ever get pregnant before I get married, I'll never have an abortion."

I hugged her tight. I knew she was profoundly impacted by the testimonies she'd heard.

> You intended to harm me, but God intended it for good to accomplish what is now being done, the saving of many lives. (Genesis 50:20 NIV)

CHAPTER 14

OPEN DOORS

Serving as a Texas state representative had not been on my bucket list. Prior to 2015, when I was sworn in during the 84th legislative session, I was heavily involved in pro-life activism. I founded two non-profit organizations, was the Texas Leader of Operation Outcry, co-hosted Faces of Abortion television show, hosted Redeemed for Life radio talk show, traveled extensively, and participated in many pro-life activities on the local, state, national and international arenas. Then, one August day in 2013, everything changed in my life through one phone call I received.

"Hello, Molly, this is John Alaniz, how are you?

"Well, John, I'm doing great. I haven't seen you in a long time. What's going on?

"I want to ask if you'd consider running against Ralph Sheffield this election cycle …?"

Everything after that sounded like he was speaking through a string phone I used to play with as a kid. For those of you too young to know what I'm talking about, kids used to tie a long, string between two paper cups and make a phone. One kid would talk through the cup while the other one would listen through the cup on the other end. To say the least, all you could hear was a muffled vibration through the string. That's all I could hear on the other end of the line. What I did hear, loud and clear, was the voice of the Lord speaking to me. Just like I heard him speak to me on July 24, 2001. The clouds didn't part, and I wasn't sitting on a rocking chair on my front porch, but I heard him in my spirit. I knew, at that moment, God had just called me to run for political office.

"What do you think, Molly? Will you consider it?"

John's voice broke through my Holy Spirit encounter. "John, I believe God just called me to run for office through you. Yes, I will. Of course, I need to pray and confirm it with the Lord, talk with my family, friends, and all my pro-life contacts and get back to you. Thank you for thinking of me."

God confirmed he was calling me to run for office. I received support from all my family, friends, and contacts. I ran against a third term incumbent and faced many challenges during the campaign. Through all the trials my campaign team and I faced, God continually reminded me to keep my eyes on the goal that laid ahead of me. We stayed upbeat and worked hard as we focused on election night when the votes came in.

One chilly, February morning while I was at the polls talking to voters, I was approached by a woman.

"Hi, I'm Molly White. How are you this morning?"

"Hi, Mrs. White. I'm a big supporter. I wanted to tell you I really appreciate your pro-life position. I read your testimony online. I had an abortion too. I've never been able to get over it. It's haunted me every day since then." For the next couple of hours, I ministered to this hurting woman in the parking lot of a polling location. She cried and shared feelings of guilt and unforgiveness toward herself. I listened and offered words of encouragement, support and love.

The following day another woman approached me. She, too, confided in me about her abortion. She, too, had been suffering in silence for over a decade. God blessed me with another opportunity to minister to and console another hurting woman in my district. These events, in my couple of months of very hard and challenging campaigning, were the most meaningful.

Finally, election night was here. I was exhausted from months of early mornings, going door to door all day long, and attending political events and rallies in the evenings. I constantly reminded myself all I had to do was survive until 10 p.m. on election night, then I could go to bed and sleep for a week. I was comforted by the thought I wouldn't have an opponent in the general election. The primary was the deciding factor of this race.

On March 4, 2014, when the votes had come in, God gave me a sound victory. I was thrilled. My family and supporters celebrated as the final counts came in. My campaign consultant called me right before the last precinct votes came in.

"Hello, this is Representative-elect Molly White."

"Hey, Molly, I know it's still early. How are the votes looking?"

"Luke, this is Representative-elect Molly White."

"Really? That's awesome. I haven't seen any updated counts yet. Congratulations. What's the lead?"

"As of now, I'm up seven-hundred plus. Just a few precincts still out, but I should win those as well."

"Fantastic. Job well done, Molly."

Sleeping in for a week was wishful thinking. I may have slept a little longer the following morning, but my phone began to ring off the hook with well wishes and congratulations. My team and I planned a victory party for all our volunteers, financial supporters, and voters. All my children and grandson attended. I was never so proud and yet, humbled by how God had moved mightily amidst all the challenges and set-backs and delivered an astounding victory over a well-funded, establishment entrenched opponent. My campaign raised and spent a mere twenty-five thousand dollars. My opponent spent ten times that much. It just goes to show, when God opens a door for us, no man can close it. (Revelation 3:8, NIV)

As a newly elected Texas State Legislator, I was invited to speak on a women's health panel with other legislators prior to the Texas Legislature convening in January 2015. The discussion was held during a public policy forum hosted by The Texas Tribune, a liberal newspaper in Austin. I had a feeling I'd be the only female pro-life speaker on the panel.

The auditorium was filled with both pro-life and pro-abortion supporters, and I recognized many pro-life leaders and advocates and could easily pick out those who were abortion supporters. My chief of staff, Hannah, was there and sat a couple of rows back with a couple of other pro-life women.

When it came time for introductions, the moderator made a deliberate attempt to delegitimize me by insinuating I was an alcoholic and drug addict, who claimed abortion hurt me. It was evident the moderator was extremely biased and an abortion rights supporter, as her introduction shows:

"Welcome to the Tribune Fest. Today, we're going to talk about Senate Bill 2 (SB 2) and its impact on women's health since it took effect this past September."

SB2 was an omnibus piece of pro-life legislation, passed through the Texas legislature in 2013 and signed into law by Governor Rick Perry. SB2 included a ban on abortions past twenty-two weeks gestation, required abortion facilities meet the same requirements as ambulatory medical centers, abortion providers to follow FDA guidelines in the administration of the RU486 abortifacient, and abortionists to have hospital admission privileges within thirty miles of their practice. All common-sense requirements.

The moderator continued, "To my far left is Representative-elect Molly White. Molly represents House District 55 in Bell County. Ms. White defeated a three-term incumbent in the

March primary. For the past fifteen years, Molly has been a pro-life leader and speaker. She struggles with alcoholism and drug addiction because of two abortions in her past. To her right is …"

What did she just say? Her voice became muffled to me, as if she were talking through miles of pipeline. The shock and disbelief how she introduced me hit me like a tsunami wave. Did she say I struggle with alcoholism and drug addiction? I see where this is going. I got a jab right out of the gate. Obviously, the moderator, a journalist with the leftist Texas Tribune, is a pro-choice feminist who's trying to discredit me. I blinked my eyes and regained my composure as the introductions were completed.

"Welcome panel and thank you for being here with us today. My first question is: SB 2 went into effect September 1 of this year and is being challenged in court to this day. Do you think SB2 has hurt women's health and access to health care here in Texas?"

I quickly sized-up the panel of speakers, Representative Susan King sat to my right, Representative Dawnna Dukes to the right of her, then Representative Carol Alvarado, and Senator Bob Duval. I concluded the senator and I were probably the only pro-lifers on the panel, and at least two out of the three other women were probably post-abortive. I didn't know Susan or Carol before our segment started. I knew Representative Dukes. She served on the State Affairs Committee where I had testified on many occasions in support of pro-life bills. She was definitely not pro-life.

I was the first one to respond to the question. Leaning forward in my chair for a clear view of the moderator, I looked directly at her and firmly stated, "First of all, I find it very offensive that you'd take words in my written testimony and twist them into a derogatory image of your view of a pro-life, post-abortive woman. I'm not, nor have I ever been, an alcoholic or drug addict."

The moderator shifted in her seat and cleared her throat. I didn't give her time to respond. I continued with my response to her question. "As the Texas Leader of Operation Outcry, representing thousands of women who regret and have been hurt by their abortions, and founder and director of Women for Life, International, I worked hard on the passage of SB2. During committee hearings, I testified in support of the bill sharing my abortion experiences." I went on to describe both my abortions. "I submitted six hundred legally admissible affidavits of Texas women who've been hurt by abortion—many of them suffering from physical complications and psychological trauma. I spoke in support of SB2, so women are not continually being subjected to shoddy abortion practices and risky health complications. I do not believe the passage of SB 2 in any way, shape, or form has hurt women's health care. The opposite is true. Making abortion clinics meet ambulatory center standards protects women's health."

Looking at the audience, I asked, "Would you rather go to an abortion clinic that is understaffed, untrained in emergency procedures, and doesn't have the proper medical equipment to handle emergencies from botched abortions or to a center that meets the medical requirements of ambulatory centers where emergencies can be taken care of immediately? Since abortion became constitutionally protected, the only thing that's changed concerning abortion procedures is the word "illegal" to "legal." Abortion is a dangerous procedure. I know many women who suffered from botched abortions and nearly lost their lives. I also know two families whose daughters died at the hands of an abortionist because he didn't know how to perform life-saving measures after he botched an abortion.

Both these young women's lives could've been saved had the abortion clinic been properly equipped and the staff trained.

"Can you imagine your daughter having an abortion without your knowledge only to be awakened in the middle of the night by a phone call from her hysterical friend who's screaming, 'They've taken Laurie to the hospital and they won't tell me anything?' The parents of this young, twenty-one-year-old woman had to drive to a different state in the wee hours of the morning only to learn their beautiful daughter was dead from a botched abortion.

"One of my dearest friends was sent home bleeding heavily after her late-term abortion. When the bleeding increased, and she started passing large clots and feeling weak, she called the Planned Parenthood clinic where the abortion was performed. They told her she was no longer their 'concern' and to go to a hospital. My friend nearly bled to death. Is this what you want for women?"

I heard a gravelly, harsh-sounding voice break in.

"I disagree. SB 2 infringes on women's access to safe and legal abortion. SB2 is nothing more than an attempt to infringe on a woman's right to choose," snapped Representative Dukes. Leaning towards the audience, she took a quick glance at me and then looked back to the audience. "Just because you became an alcoholic and drug addict after your abortion doesn't mean you speak for women."

Representative Dukes's remarks got some cheers from some women in the audience, but it was a direct stab at me to try and shut me up. That confirms my suspicion about Dawnna Dukes. She's post-abortive, and there are the post-abortive women in the audience. I was able to identify them because my comments rubbed some wounds, resulting in a strong reaction from the hurting. Dukes continued to deride me and defend abortion. Her haughty, self-righteous disguise didn't fool me nor intimidate me. I decided to press her.

"Don't you dare judge me. This is my experience, my story. Unless you've had an abortion, you have no idea how one impacts a woman."

Plopping back in her chair, Dukes threw up her arms and blurted out, "Okay, in front of God and everyone, I had an abortion. There, I said it. My abortion didn't bother me. The reason I haven't told anyone before now is it's a private matter, nobody's business." She glanced back at me and in a condescending tone, continued her attack, "I didn't turn into an alcoholic or drug addict. It was my choice, my body. To this day, I don't regret it. It only made me stronger. I'm raising a ten-year-old daughter I adopted as an infant and have been battling uterine cancer while at the same time as serving as a state representative. I can attest having a biopsy of my uterus is riskier than having an abortion. I'm in no way weak because I had an abortion." She sat back in her seat and looked victoriously at the women in the audience who were cheering her on.

She had just shared her testimony of how abortion hurt her and she's clueless. She doesn't even recognize the symptoms. Denial is the first clue. Obviously, she's either suffering from infertility or needed a replacement baby without getting pregnant, and she's battling uterine cancer, two health risks of abortion. She's angry and defensive and still in the justification stage, which are classic mental health issues of abortion.

The other members of the panel and the moderator sat quietly trying to hide their uncomfortable feelings. Senator Duval, a medical doctor, finally broke in and challenged Dawnna's claim that a biopsy was riskier than abortion. She became irritated and snapped back at the Senator, "Abortion is a safe medical procedure and safer than childbirth." That evoked a strong reaction from the senator. By this point in our twenty-five-minute panel discussion, the moderator had lost control of the discussion. I continued speaking in support of the various aspects of SB2, and Dawnna challenged every talking point.

Trying to stay on time and regain some type of control of the discussion, the moderator piped in and said, "This has been an interesting discussion. Time is about up. What would you like to say in conclusion to our topic of SB2?"

I'm glad you asked. I want these pro-abortion women to know they don't fool me. I leaned forward, looked at Dukes, and then at the group of pro-abortion women in the audience. "Twenty years ago, I'd be sitting out there with a lot of you defending abortion, because I had to defend my own abortions. If I couldn't defend them, then I'd have to face the fact that abortion killed my babies. At that time, I didn't know there was a merciful and forgiving God who was bigger than my guilt and able to handle my pain. The bravest thing I've ever done, and any woman can do, is face the truth—abortion killed our children and made us an accomplice to murder. It's unnatural for we women to kill our own defenseless children. That's the reason abortion hurts women physically, psychologically, emotionally, and spiritually. Now, I'm free from the bondage of abortion. I've been saved, delivered, and healed and so can you."

That was it. Time was up. The moderator thanked all of us on the panel and the audience for coming and dismissed us. Representative Susan King thanked me for sharing my testimony.

"Wow, that got a little tense."

I shook her hand, "It does when women are still in denial and don't like it when their wounds are rubbed."

Later, she and I would have lengthy discussions where I dispelled her rationale for abortion. She was a nurse, and though she said she'd never have an abortion, she felt there were certain compelling cases where a woman should be able to choose. I was able to speak truth into each scenario, changing her mind and her thought process.

After the panel discussion, several members of the audience came to me and thanked me for sharing so boldly. I kept my eye on the whereabouts of Representative Dukes. I felt compassion for her and wanted to keep the line of communication open between us. Several people were talking to her, so I waited patiently. I knew she saw me hanging around and glancing at her from time to time. I think she was trying to stall the confrontation because most of the people around her appeared to be members of her staff. Finally, I had an opening to approach her.

I reached out my hands towards her, indicating I wasn't in a combative mode. "Representative Dukes, I want you to know I have no hard feelings toward you." I could feel the wall of tension around her. She looked surprised I was offering to make peace with her. "I'm sorry to hear you're battling with uterine cancer. I'll make it a point to pray for you."

Trying to blow me off, she smugly responded, "Oh, I believe in Jesus. I pray to him all the time."

"That's good. I just wanted you to know I'm committed to pray for you, and I look forward to serving with you this upcoming legislative session." I reached out to shake her hand, she offered a limp grip, which I took with a warm and firm grasp. I decided to make my goodbye a bit personal: "It was nice to meet you, Dawnna."

Representative Dukes was absent most of the 2015 Session. When my staff brought to my attention Dawnna had been sick, I wrote a note to her and sent it to her staff to deliver. I told Dawnna we missed seeing her during session, and my staff and I were praying for her speedy recovery. I included the following Scripture from Jeremiah 17:14: "Heal me, LORD, and I will be healed; save me and I will be saved, for you are the one I praise."

A couple of weeks later, when we were ready to debate and vote on the Appropriations Bill, I noticed Dawnna up front on the House floor. She glanced to the back of the room and saw me. It was as if she knew where I sat and had been looking for me. Here she came, headed directly toward me. Dawnna's desk was on the second row from the front. Mine was the second row from the back. Her eyes were fixed on me. Her pace was quick. She covered the distance in no time. Oh, boy. This could be interesting. I wonder what's on her mind.

Without slowing her pace, she walked up to me, threw her arms around my shoulders, and gave me a long, firm, bear hug. I couldn't believe this was happening. After a few seconds the shock wore off and I hugged her back.

She pulled away, put her hands on my shoulders, and looking at me in square in the eye said, "Thank you for sending me that kind note. It really meant a lot to me. You're the only one who reached out to me since I've been absent. Back and neck injuries I got in a car wreck have kept me bedridden. I've been in a tremendous amount of pain. My heart was touched when my staff brought me your note. It meant a lot to me. Thank you for thinking of me."

We hugged again and walked toward the front of the House floor where debates were taking place. I was about to present an amendment on the school finance portion of the Appropriations Bill. My amendment laid out ground rules for sex education that followed a federal guideline requiring all sex education in Texas to follow abstinence until marriage principles. Dawnna and I stood next to each other listening to members present pros and cons of the bill.

Then I whispered, "My amendment is up next, Dawnna. I'll talk to you later."

Her head popped back. She looked at me, surprised this freshman legislator was presenting an amendment.

"What's your amendment?"

I told her the short version as I walked to the microphone.

"Boy, it doesn't take you long to jump in the fire does it?" she said as she folded her arms across her chest.

My encounter with Dawnna that day was a reminder that God commands us to love our enemies. Proverbs 25:21 (NIV) says, "If your enemy is hungry, give him food to eat, and if he is thirsty, give him water to drink. For in so doing, you will heap burning coals on his head, and the LORD will reward you." Ms. Dukes was hungry for recognition, and the Lord prompted me to give it to her. She was thirsty for validation, and I quenched it with the word of God.

> When they bring you before the synagogues and the rulers and the authorities, do not worry about how or what you are to speak in your defense, or what to say; for the Holy Spirit will teach you and in that very hour what you ought to say. (Luke 12:11–12 NASB)

CHAPTER 15

The Power of Testimony

There's no telling how my life would've turned out if it hadn't been for a stranger witnessing to me about the saving grace of Jesus during a time I struggled with depression, guilt, and shame from my abortions. I may have become a pro-choice advocate and in a state of psychological dysfunction of denial, justification, and rationalization, while desperately trying to defend "my choice" as a way to ease my conscious and spirit. My marriage may have ended in divorce. My relationships with my parents could have been severed. I could be living in secrecy keeping my abortions buried deep within my heart and living life with a mask on and acting as if everything was wonderful in my life. Thank God for his infinite grace, mercy, and love, which pulled me out of the depths of sin, despair, and bondage and restored my crippled mind and spirit.

When we allow God to use our pain for his purpose, he will use us in ways we've never imagined—like calling me to run for State Representative in Texas. I was not the most qualified. I'd never held a political office before. The only expertise I had was in pro-life work and activism. I walked through a door God had opened for me with one goal—advance the kingdom of God, defend the Biblical worldview, and to learn and grow in that position. As a state representative I tried my best to represent Jesus.

After losing reelection, I stumbled spiritually. I couldn't understand why God would call me to run for office for just one term. After months of questioning, soul searching, and seeking the Lord, I realized he gave me the opportunity as a tool for my future pro-life endeavors. As a former state representative, I have access to people and places that would've been more difficult otherwise. God puts us in places to use us, teach us, and prepare us for the next assignment he has for us. If we miss out of a developmental stage, we won't be prepared for the next door he opens for us. But the most important thing God revealed to me is from that experience, my relationship with my parents grew closer and deeper than I could ever have hoped for or imagined. That's the biggest blessing.

Being saved, delivered, and healed is not the end all in our lives as followers of Christ. God commands us to comfort those who are hurting with the same comfort we ourselves received (2 Corinthians 1:4). We must reach out to women and men hurting from an abortion decision, lead them to Christ, and encourage them to seek healing. How do we do reach this population? Through the power of testimony.

Jesus used the power of testimony when he was teaching his disciples. The disciples used the power of testimony when they were witnessing about Jesus. It was the power of testimony Mary and the other women used to tell the disciples Jesus's tomb was empty. It's the power of testimony that convinced his followers Jesus rose from the dead and sits at the right hand of the Father. It's the power of testimony that leads us to our Savior. It's the power of testimony that exposes the schemes of the devil and gives God the glory. It's abortion testimonies that expose the works of the devil, change hearts, comfort those who are hurting, set the captives free, and change public policy.

Sharing our stories about what led to our abortion decision, what the experience was like, how the decision impacted our life touches the human heart, and helps those who have had the same experience identify with us. Sharing about God's love, grace, and mercy, which led to our salvation and healing gives the wounded hope they, too, can be saved, delivered, and healed.

Have you had an abortion? Were you involved in an abortion decision? Did my story stir up hidden memories and feelings? Are you ready to be healed? I encourage you to take the bold step that will change your life for the better. Do it for yourself. Do it for your family. I can bear witness—a hurting woman has a hurting family. A healed woman has a healed family. When you heal from the trauma of abortion, your family will heal from the consequences of abortion trauma.

If you're ready, I invite you to attend an abortion recovery Bible study. Every pro-life pregnancy center, and many churches, offer free abortion recovery programs in private settings. These programs range from weekly group studies to weekend retreats. They are free of charge (you may have to pay for the materials) and completely confidential. Retreats are available to women, men, and related family members who've lost a child through abortion. Be sure it's a Christ-centered abortion recovery and not an imposter some abortion clinics provide. These are designed to make abortion look good and your feelings not related to your abortion.

There are also abortion recovery programs designed just for men. Many men prefer to do a one-on-one with another man who leads the study or by themselves. Men have many options to best suit their individual needs.

Every post-abortive woman and man I've encouraged to go through recovery did not regret it. Some took more convincing than others. Years ago, I was a guest on the Joni Lamb show called Table Talk and the Joni and Marcus Show on Daystar Television. I shared my testimony and talked about ending abortion. The next day, I got a call from a distraught woman from Illinois. She'd watched the show and was compelled to contact me and share her abortion experience. I listened, I consoled, I empathized, and I prayed for her. This precious woman had aborted out of fear of being judged but had lived in consuming fear of judgment for years afterwards.

Her voice trembled as she choked out the words, "You don't understand. My mother-in-law is the director of our local crisis pregnancy center. She and the ladies there will judge me. I can't go there. I live in a small town. Everyone will know."

"Is there a center you can contact in a nearby town?"

"They'll know my mother-in-law too."

"My sweet friend, abortion recovery programs are completely confidential and private. No one is going to reveal who is in the groups."

"I can't. I just can't," she sobbed.

"How about looking up a weekend retreat? They're held in undisclosed locations. They're only three days long."

After days of talking, ministering, and convincing, she agreed to go to the next available retreat. Her life was transformed. The shackles of shame, regret, and guilt were broken. We became best friends. God opened the door for her to speak, preach, evangelize, minister, and get politically involved. The enemy tried to keep her silent, in bondage to fear, but once she allowed God to take her on the healing journey, Satan no longer had a grip on her. She's been a kingdom activist ever since. If you can relate to this story, please attend an abortion recovery program and receive freedom from captivity. God has big plans for you. Don't allow any fear to keep you bound anymore.

Once you've gone through recovery, and are mentally, emotionally, and spiritually ready, allow the Lord to use your testimony for good. Legislators need to hear our stories to help them understand abortions' long term impact, so they can make wise decisions on abortion-related legislation. Pastors need to hear our stories, so they will understand the impact abortion is having on the Christian community and be stirred into action. Young people need to hear our stories, so they won't be deceived and make a life-taking, life-altering choice. The hurting world needs to hear our stories of how abortion nearly destroyed us and how God saved and healed us. What an evangelistic tool to use when we relate what Satan used against us, God uses for his kingdom purposes. (Genesis 50:20)

Most importantly, ask the Lord to open doors to use you and your experience for his glory. Then, get a passport and a sturdy set of luggage. When we surrender our lives to be used by God, he could send us all around the world. He's done that for me, and I know he can do that for you.

Sharing our testimonies in public and private settings is the most powerful thing we can do for the pro-life movement. Testimony exposes the lies we believed, changes hearts, educates the uniformed, and affects public policy decisions. Our testimonies always produce good fruit. I've been sharing my testimony for more than twenty years. At first, it was difficult, like when I flew to Washington, DC, with Allan Parker and shared at the Shake the Nation Back to Life media event. My emotions were still raw. I struggled with fear of rejection and condemnation. I was angry at the injustice of abortion, and I was defensive. God eventually delivered me of all that.

Each time I shared my story, God would show me an area of woundedness I wasn't aware of and take me further along in my healing journey. For example, one day I was a guest on the Wiley Drake Show online radio program. The host and I had a great discussion on the ills of abortion when he asked me a question I'd never been asked or thought of before.

"Molly, what was the door that opened that led you to having an abortion and your downward spiral?"

Instantly, and to my surprise, the Lord showed me the root of what eventually led me to an abortion clinic. "When I lost my virginity during a date rape while I was in high school. My boyfriend wanted sex, and I didn't. He was determined, and I was unable to fight off his advances. Afterwards, I felt dirty and ashamed. I thought no decent man would want to marry me because I was no longer innocent. That date rape damaged my self-worth and self-esteem. Our relationship was damaged, and we eventually broke up. I figured the only way I'd be able to keep a boyfriend was to have sex. But sex is not the glue to a relationship, especially out of wedlock. In fact, sex is not love and love is not sex. My low self-esteem and worth combined with my sexually promiscuous lifestyle is what led to pregnancy outside of marriage and making me easy prey for the abortion industry."

I couldn't believe that came out of my mouth. It was a revelation only the Holy Spirit could pinpoint and expose. After the interview was over, I began doing some soul searching. The Lord showed me how not only did my date rape damage my femininity, it also damaged my ability to be fully intimate with my spouse.

Abortion is like a rape. A woman is in a vulnerable position and a male doctor (or female) is between her legs and performing a procedure that is violating, painful, and degrading. I prayed and sought the Lord to heal me and restore those things that should come naturally to a woman. That's just one example of the many ways the Lord has healed me throughout the past twenty years of sharing about my abortions.

Now, I can share my testimony in two to three minutes or an hour depending on the time frame I have. I, and countless other post-abortive women, have shared our testimonies to support pro-life legislation and defend legal challenges against pro-life laws. We've shared our testimonies to educate lawmakers, students, ambassadors, heads of nations, ministry leaders, and the general public. We've shared our stories in debates to counter the lies and deceptive propaganda of pro-choice supporters. Our testimonies have saved lives, generations even, and healed the broken hearted. Your story is vital in advancing the kingdom of God and in defending the Biblical worldview. I invite you to join the victorious overcomers of the trauma of abortion and add your voice to ours.

If you haven't had an abortion, you've been educated on some of the deceptive practices of the abortion industry and abortions' long reaching, life damaging consequences. God can use your compassion toward those who're hurting and to educate others.

Prayer is the most important activity you can do. Commit to praying once a day for the end of abortion. Join or create a local prayer group, which focuses on abortion. Participate in the annual Life Chain on the first Sunday of every October. I've led local Life Chains for the past decade. Participants gather at a highly visible location, hold pro-life signs, and pray for just one hour for the end of abortion.

I've witnessed dozens of positive responses from our presence. Women stop and approach me or others to share their stories with us. We pray with them and connect them to a recovery program. Others join us after driving by and seeing our signs. I've witnessed some nasty reactions from some people too. These reactions often stem from a guilty conscience. I always pray for their salvation and healing.

Participate in the annual 40 Days for Life campaign. Participants commit to pray outside an abortion facility during a forty-day period. Hundreds of lives have been saved and pregnant women spared from the trauma of abortion during these events.

I remember one time when I was praying at a local abortion clinic during a 40 Days for Life campaign, God moved in an unexpected way. I'd been praying for several weeks during my weekly time slot to no avail. Women and girls slipped through my fingers as they walked into the abortion clinic. During my prayer, I cried out to God. Father God, I've been faithful to come here and pray for babies and their mothers to be saved from abortion week after week, year after year. I've been faithfully serving you for years, being obedient to what you've called me to do. Can't you give me one life? Just one, so that I know I'm doing the right thing. Please God, let me see some fruit of my labor. In the mighty name of your son, Jesus, I pray, amen. My prayer time at the clinic was done. No one listened to my offers for help. No minds were changed, no lives were saved. I packed up my sign and went home.

God did answer my prayer that day in front of the abortion clinic. Not visibly on the sidewalk, but when I got back to my office. I received a phone call, which led to the saving of a baby and his mother. The caller told me he called the abortion clinic the very hour I was there praying. He was checking on the costs of abortions. He mistook my phone book listing as an abortion clinic. I was able to minster to this man and his girlfriend. He was convinced to be a man and protect and provide for his child. She was not convinced to give her child life. After many weeks of her texting me all her justifications for having an abortion and me countering all her excuses, the Holy Spirit led me to ask this tormented young woman a question that changed everything.

"Do you want to know how to get your peace back?"

She responded, "How?"

"By deciding to do what is right. Once you decide to do what is right, giving your baby life, you will open the doors for God to come in, provide for your needs, and work miracles on your behalf and your child's. Right now, you're blocking the Holy Spirit from moving. Trust the Lord. You won't regret it."

Once she chose life, her peace was restored, and God moved mightily in her life. Was it perfect? No. Did her boyfriend step up to the plate? No. Her family and church stepped up to the plate and helped her. She's a happy mother of a beautiful little boy with no regrets.

God does answer prayers. Not always in our timing. Not always the way we visualize the answers, but he does answer in his timing, in his way, and for his purpose.

Allow God to use you as an answer to prayer. There are all kinds of pro-life activities you can get involved in. Offer help and support to pregnant, unwed mothers. Start abortion recovery class in your church or community. Volunteer at a pregnancy resource center, donate to pro-life, non-profit organizations. Sign pro-life petitions. Vote for pro-life political and judicial candidates. Run for office. Be silent no more.

Encourage your pastor to talk about this issue. During Sanctity of Life Sunday, encourage your pastor to reach out to women, men, and extended family who're hurting from abortion. Give them an opportunity to come forward for prayer and ministry. I approached my pastor to do just that years ago.

My church fully embraced the biblical worldview of life and participated in the yearly event. One year, I got permission and support from my pastor to do something different than our normal routine on this occasion. I felt led to make this Sanctity of Life Sunday more personal and meaningful for my fellow church members. I bought dozens of pink and blue carnations. I gave one to each member as they came into the sanctuary. Pastor Mike ended his sermon early to give time for our special service. He taught on what God's word said concerning life and explained to the body we were going to have group participation in an informal memorial service for the millions of children who'd been aborted.

"Ladies and gentlemen, the pink and blue carnations Molly handed out this morning represent baby girls and boys who've lost their lives through abortion. In a few minutes, I will invite you to come to the altar, lay down your flower, and say a silent prayer on behalf of the children who were aborted and have never been mourned. Molly has something she'd like to say before we get started. Come to the front, Molly."

I made my way to Pastor Mike, took the microphone he handed to me, and faced my church family. "Y'all know about my abortions, and I'm actively involved in pro-life work. As we were preparing for this Sunday, the Lord impressed upon me and Pastor Mike to offer those who've lost a child to abortion, miscarriage, still birth, or as an infant to please come forward, and let us pray for you and grieve with you. We want all of you to know, we care about you and your sorrow. While we're praying for those who come forward, the rest of you can come up, place your flowers on the altar, and pray as the Spirit leads you. You may leave after that if you need to."

The ministry time was moving. Many came forward. There was weeping, confessions, and ministry. The Holy Spirit moved powerfully throughout this time. Many began their healing journeys. God used that event to change our church for the better. Congregants were more compassionate towards each other and freer to be open with their struggles and pain. It was beautiful and an honor to be part of.

We, as followers of Christ and as a nation, cannot remain silent when it comes to the injustice of abortion. We cannot continue allowing pregnant women and girls to be led away to the death chambers of the abortion clinics. We cannot be deaf to the silent cries of those who're living in bondage from their abortions. We must do something. "Then I heard the voice of the Lord saying, 'Whom shall I send? And who will go for us?' And I said, 'Here am I. Send me!'" (Isaiah 6:8 NIV). Do you hear the Lord speaking to you? Will you answer his call?

And they overcame him because of the blood of the Lamb and because of the word of their testimony, and they did not love their life even when faced with death. (Revelation 12:11 NASB)

SYMPTOMS OF POST ABORTION STRESS

EMOTIONAL SYMPTOMS

Guilt
Unable to forgive herself
Emotionally numb
Shame
Sorrow
Unworthiness
Self-condemnation
Feels degraded/debased
Anger
Depression
Anxiety
Loneliness
Bitterness
Confusion
Fears God's punishment
Fears losing a child
Remorse
Grief
Hopelessness
Helplessness
Rage
Anguish
Panic
Frustration
Feels exploited
Self-hatred
Despair
Regret
Feels isolated/alienated

Feels rejected
Horror
Flashbacks/nightmares
Fears another pregnancy
Feels inferior
Preoccupation with due date or anniversary date
Secretive

BEHAVIORAL CHANGES

Abusive
Withdrawn
Over-protective of living children
Avoids baby reminders
Marital stress
Crying spells
Sleep disturbances
Develops eating disorders
Self-punishing or self-degrading behavior
Alcohol/drug abuse
Wants atonement/replacement child
Changes in relationships
Difficulty with intimacy
Loss of interest in sex
Promiscuity or frigidity
Suicidal impulses
Tolerates abusive relationships
Reduced motivation
Loss of normal sources of pleasure
Fails to bond with subsequent children
Divides time into "before" and "after" abortion
Damaged relationships with living children [1]

SPIRITUAL EFFECTS OF ABORTION

Sin and separation from God
Broken relationships
Unforgiving heart towards self & others
Mercilessness
Fear of discipline from the Father
Roots of bitterness
Anger towards self, God & others
Foothold for the enemy or demonic oppression
Hopelessness
Inability to receive God's forgiveness
Prideful judgment
Fruitlessness
Works over grace
Shame & secrecy

COPING MECHANISMS

Coping is an activity we do to seek and apply solutions to stressful situations or problems that emerge because of our stressors. Actually, the term "coping" is more associated with "reactive coping," because in general, we see coping as a response to a stressor. There's also what we call "proactive coping," wherein the coping response is aimed at preventing a possible encounter with a future stressor. (I have seen examples of proactive coping from an abortion experience that included women having their tubes tied, or men having vasectomies to prevent another pregnancy and the possibility of another abortion, and post-abortive women and men becoming lesbians or homosexuals to avoid pregnancy and another abortion.) There are some types of coping mechanisms which are maladaptive. Some psychologists say that maladaptive coping is also synonymous to "non-coping," since a person who responds to a stressor using a coping mechanism but isn't able to positively ward off the stressor or solve the stressful situation hasn't coped with the stress at all. 2

MALADAPTIVE COPING MECHANISMS

Denial is the most common coping mechanism. Denial involves the change of mindset or a revision of thoughts.

Defense—the unconscious ways of coping stress. Examples: reaction formation, regression

Adaptive—tolerates the stress. Examples: altruism, symbolization

Avoidance—keeps self away from the stress. Examples: denial, dissociation, fantasy, passive aggression, reaction formation.

Attack—diverts one's consciousness to a person or group of individuals other than the stressor or the stressful situation. Examples: displacement, emotionality, projection.

Behavioral—modifies the way we act in order to minimize or eradicate the stress. Examples: compensation, sublimation, undoing.

Cognitive—alters the way we think so that stress is reduced or removed. Examples: compartmentalization, intellectualization, rationalization, repression, suppression.

Self-harm—intends to harm self as a response to stress. Examples: introjection, self-harming

Conversion—changes one thought, behavior or emotion into another. Example: somatization. [3]

IMPACT (OF ABORTION) ON MOTHER/CHILD RELATIONSHIP

Abortion severely damages the mother's ability to form healthy relationships with her living children. Following is a list of common types of problems:

Image of self as a mother is changed. I don't feel like a mother. She cannot believe herself a real mother when she has killed her own child.

Failure to bond with their children. Some are afraid God will punish her by taking her child if she loves him too much. Another says it would be unfair to the child she killed to love the living children. Others may view themselves as unworthy. Some withdraw from their families and do not mother at all.

Bonding with children in unhealthy ways. She becomes controlling, overprotective, and clinging, often refusing to let anyone else hold the child. She may have difficulty being separated from the child for even a very short time.

Attempting to replace the aborted child with a new baby. She places high expectations on the new child to meet her deep emotional needs. However, with each new baby the emptiness remains. She may not love her children because they have not filled the emptiness, but she keeps believing the next one will. Some even believe erroneously that the spirit of the dead child is in the new baby. [4]

ABORTION PROCEDURES & RISKS

First Trimester Abortions—During the first trimester (through 13 weeks of gestation) an abortion can be performed through medicine or surgery.

Medical (Nonsurgical) Abortion—

Medical abortion uses medicine to end a pregnancy instead of surgery and is used early in pregnancy—70 days (10 weeks) or less from the first day of your last menstrual period. This method requires several visits to your doctor. The medicines used for a medical abortion cause bleeding, cramping and passing of the fetus and other tissue. In some cases, excessive bleeding may require blood transfusions, treatment with medication, surgery or saline transfusions. Severe infection is a known risk following a medical abortion.

Possible complications of a medical abortion using mifepristone and misoprostol pills:

In about every 4 of 100 procedures, medications are needed to control bleeding.

About 1 of every 100 procedures will require a surgical procedure to stop bleeding and to remove parts of the baby and the placenta.

In up to 5 of every 1,000 procedures, blood transfusions will be administered.

Failure to remove all parts of the baby and other tissue, including the placenta, may require a follow-up surgical procedure.

Increased risk of infertility (the inability to have a baby) may result if complications occur with the procedure.

Less than 3 percent of procedures will not work and will result in a surgical procedure to end the pregnancy or complete the abortion.

2 of every 1,000 procedures, serious bacterial infections have been reported.

Rarely, severe infection after a medical abortion has resulted in death.

More than 15 out of every 100 women with a medical abortion will experience nausea, weakness, fever/chills, vomiting, headache, diarrhea, or dizziness.

About 3 to 5 of every procedure result in a visit to the emergency room.

In up to 6 of every 1,000 procedures, hospitalization related to medical abortion will be required.

Hemorrhaging (heavy bleeding) may occur. [5]

SURGICAL ABORTIONS—

FIRST TRIMESTER

Dilation & Curettage (D&C) With Vacuum Aspiration— The doctor first opens (dilates) the cervix and then empties the uterus with suction. After suctioning, the doctor may scrape the walls of the uterus to make sure the unborn child, placenta, and contents of the uterus have been completely removed. Possible side effects and risks include: cramping of the uterus or pelvic pain; a hole in the uterus (uterine perforation) or other damage to the uterus; injury to the bowel or the bladder; a cut or torn cervix (cervical laceration); incomplete removal of the unborn child, placenta, or contents of the uterus requiring an additional operation; infection; complications from anesthesia such as respiratory problems, nausea and vomiting, headaches, or drug reactions; inability to get pregnant due to infection or complication from an operation; possible hysterectomy as a result of complication or injury during the procedure; hemorrhage (heavy bleeding); emergency treatment for any of the above problems, including possible need to treat with an operation, medicines, or a blood transfusion; rarely, death.

SECOND TRIMESTER ABORTIONS (13 WEEKS TO 22 WEEKS)

Dilation & Evacuation (D&E)—To prepare for the procedure, the doctor will open (dilate) the cervix. Most women experience some pain, so the doctor may give you a painkiller —either locally by shots in the area of the cervix or by a general anesthetic—or a sedative (which will leave you conscious). The uterus will be scraped, and the unborn child and placenta are removed. After sixteen weeks, the unborn child and placenta are removed, piece-by-piece, using forceps or other instruments. This procedure will take less than an hour. Possible side effects and risks include: hole in the uterus (uterine perforation) or other damage to the uterus; injury to the bowel or bladder; cut or torn cervix (cervical laceration); incomplete removal of the unborn child, placenta, or contents of the uterus requiring an additional operation; infection; complications from anesthesia, such as respiratory problems, nausea and vomiting, headaches, or drug reactions; inability to get pregnant due to infection or complication from an operation; possible hysterectomy as a result of complication or injury during the procedure; hemorrhage (heavy bleeding); emergency treatment for any of the above problems, including the possible need to treat with an operation, medicines, or a blood transfusion; rarely, death.

THIRD TRIMESTER ABORTIONS (22 WEEKS AND BEYOND. NOTE: THIRD TRIMESTER ABORTIONS ARE ILLEGAL IN MANY STATES.)

Abortion by Labor Induction (Medical Induction)— Medicines will be used to start labor. These medicines can be put in the vagina, injected in the uterus (womb) or given into the vein (intravenously or by IV). The medicines used cause the uterus to contract and labor to begin. Sometimes more than one medicine will be used. This procedure may take from several hours to several days. Your doctor may use instruments to scrape the uterus and make sure that the unborn child, placenta, and other contents of the uterus have been completely removed. Possible side effects and risks include: nausea or vomiting; diarrhea; fever; infection; complications from anesthesia such as respiratory problems, nausea and vomiting, headaches, or drug reactions; inability to get pregnant due to infection or complication from an operation; possible hysterectomy as a result of complication or injury during the procedure; damage or rupture of the uterus (womb); the possibility of a live-born baby; incomplete removal of the unborn child, placenta, or contents of the uterus requiring an operation; hemorrhage (heavy bleeding); water intoxication; emergency treatment for any of the above problems, including the possible need to treat with an operation, medicines, or a blood transfusion; rarely, death.

Dilation and Extraction (D&X)—The doctor will dilate (open) the cervix. The doctor will grasp the unborn child's foot with an instrument and deliver the child except for the head. While the head is kept in the birth canal, scissors are used to make a hole in the back of the head, a tube is inserted, and suction is applied. The contents of the unborn child's skull are suctioned out, the bones of the head collapse, and the child is delivered dead. Possible side effects and risks include: a hole in the uterus (uterine perforation) or other damage to the uterus; injury to the bowel or bladder; cut or torn cervix (cervical laceration); incomplete removal of the unborn child, placenta, or contents of the uterus, requiring an additional operation; infection; complications from anesthesia such as respiratory problems, nausea and vomiting, headaches, or drug reactions; inability to get pregnant due to infection or complication from an operation; possible hysterectomy as a result of complication or injury during the procedure; hemorrhage (heavy bleeding); emergency treatment for any of the above problems, including the possible need to treat with an operation, medicines, or a blood transfusion; rarely, death.

LEGAL ABORTION INCREASES VIOLENCE AGAINST WOMEN

Since the legalization of abortion on demand in America, violence against pregnant women has increased. Research shows that pregnant women are at increased risk of being physically attacked or murdered.

Homicide has become the leading cause of death among pregnant women.

In many cases, women were assaulted or killed for refusing to abort or because the attacker did not want the baby.

A high percentage of women who experienced violence while pregnant reported being punched or kicked in the abdomen, usually by the father of the unborn baby.

Many women experience abortion as a serious trauma and develop post-traumatic stress disorder. A study at a South African clinic found that 18% of their patients developed post-traumatic stress disorder after aborting. [6]

Does Legalizing Abortion Protect Women's Health?

In the developed world, the decline in maternal mortality rates coincided "with the development of obstetric techniques and improvement in the general health status of women" (from 1935 to the 1950s), according to World Health Organization. This took place well before the widespread legalization of abortion.

According to the United Nations Population Division (UNPD), there has been no substantial decrease in maternal mortality or child mortality since the 1994 International Conference on Population and Development in Cairo and the 1995 Fourth World Conference on Women in Beijing. This is true even though, in that same period, more women have had access to legal abortion than ever before. [7]

Hidden Dangers of Birth Control and Contraceptives

Combined Oral Contraceptives (YAZ, etc.)Side effects include heart attacks, strokes, blood clots in the legs, lungs, heart, or brain, high blood pressure, liver tumors, gallstones, change in sex drive, and yellowing of the skin or eyes (jaundice).

Progestin-Only Pills

Side effects include irregular menstrual bleeding, ovarian cysts, depression, weight gain, decreased libido, headaches, breast tenderness, fatigue, and acne.

Depo-Provera (Birth Control Shot)

Side effects include increased risk of breast cancer, heart attacks, depression, blood clots, osteoporosis, hair loss or increased hair on the face or body, severe chest pain, decreased libido, severe pelvic pain, sudden numbness, and abnormally heavy menstrual bleeding.

Ortho Evra (Birth Control Patch)

Side effects include heart attacks, strokes, blood clots in the legs, lungs, heart, or brain, high blood pressure, liver tumors, gallstones, change in sex drive, and yellowing of the skin or eyes (jaundice).

NuvaRing (Birth Control Vaginal Ring)

Side effects include heart attacks, strokes, blood clots in the legs, lungs, heart, or brain, thrombophlebitis and venous thrombosis with or without embolism, arterial thromboembolism, pulmonary embolism, myocardial infarction, cerebral hemorrhage, cerebral thrombosis, hypertension, hepatic adenomas, high blood pressure, liver tumors, gallstones, change in sex drive, and yellowing of the skin or eyes jaundice).

Implanon (Birth Control Implant)

Side effects include depression, ovarian cysts, weight gain, heavy menstrual bleeding, depersonalization, breast pain, change in sex drive, insomnia, vaginal discharge, back pain, and irritability.

Plan B One-Step (Levonorgestrel)

Side effects include dizziness, fatigue, breast tenderness, headaches, heavier menstrual bleeding, lower abdominal pain, and nausea.

ellaOne

Molly S. White

Side effects include hives, dry mouth, kidney stones, hot flashes, attention deficit, swollen tongue, acid reflux, blurred vision, depression, anxiety, menstrual disorders, constipation, trembling, infection, dehydration, renal pain, and nose bleeds.

RU-486, Mifeprex, Mifegyne (Mifepristone)

Side effects include severe and potentially fatal infections and heavy bleeding, uterine cramping, spotting, blood clots, passing of tissue, persistent fever, severe abdominal pain, and syncope (temporary loss of consciousness or fainting). 8

HOPE AND HEALING RESOURCES

Operation Outcry
https://www.operationoutcry.org/hope-and-healing/
Abortion Recovery International
http://www.abortionrecovery.org/

PREGNANCY RESOURCE CENTERS

CareNet—https://www.care-net.org/what-is-a-pregnancy-center/
Heartbeat International—
https://www.heartbeatinternational.org/
Center Against Forced Abortion—
http://thejusticefoundation.org/cafa/

REFERENCES

1. Judy Cooter, Carolyn Rice and Jeannie Stoner, Facilitating Biblical Healing, South Carolina, Piedmont's Women's Center, 2002, 17.

2. Sarah Mae Sincero, Stress and Coping Mechanisms, Accessed July 8, 2019, https://explorable.com/stress-and-coping-mechanisms, Nov 13, 2012.

3. Judy Cooter, Carolyn Rice and Jeannie Stoner, Facilitating Biblical Healing, 18-19.

4. A Woman's Right to Know, Informational Material, Revised December 2016, Texas Department of State Health Services, https://www.dshs.state.tx.us/wrtk/default.shtm, 14.

5. A Woman's Right to Know, Informational Material, Texas Department of State Health Services, 16-17.

6. Legal Abortions Increases Violence Against Women, Women 4 Life, http://women-4-life.org/legal-abortion-increases-violence-against-women.

7. Does Legalizing Abortion Protect Women's Health? (2009) National Right to Life Educational Trust Fund. Accessed July 11, 2019 https://www.nrlc.org/uploads/international/MMEnglsh.pdf

8. Melissa Nehsdal & Pam Stenzel, Nobody Told Me, What You Need to Know About the Physical and Emotional Consequences of Sex Outside of Marriage, Grand Rapids, MI, Revell, 2010

ABOUT THE AUTHOR

Molly White is a former Texas State Representative in House District 55. Prior to running for office, she was a pro-life, grassroots activist, public speaker, and published author. From 2001 to the present day, Molly serves as the Texas Leader of Operation Outcry, a project of the Justice Foundation. The founder and director of Redeemed for Life Ministries and Women for Life International, she has been a co-host on "Faces of Abortion" television show and the host of the "Redeemed for Life" radio talk show.

Molly White has appeared on numerous national and international television shows, news stations, documentaries, and press conferences. Her expertise on pro-life issues has resulted in invitations to speak at Christian, political, civic, and medical events all over the United States and in seven different countries.

She has led the largest pro-life delegations to the United Nations Commission on the Status of Women conferences and has attended the UN Conference on Population and the World Conference on Youth both in New York and Geneva, Switzerland. During these events, Molly met with heads of nations, political leaders, Christian leaders, and hundreds of women leaders to talk about the importance of defending life, motherhood, marriage, and families. Her work has led to the passage of dozens of pro-life laws in Texas and Washington, DC, and the defeat of measures that would hurt lives and families.

White's most rewarding work is leading people to Christ and ministering to countless hurting men and women all around the world, including on the floor of the House of Representatives.

She is the recipient of the Faces of Courage Award by Texans for Life, the Defender of Life Award, the 2016 Civitas Award by the Justice Foundation, and the Prolife Champion Award for the 84th Legislative Session by Texas Right to Life.

Molly graduated from the University of Mary Hardin-Baylor with a degree in psychology. She has been married to Ronald White for thirty years. Together they have three children and six beautiful, sweet, adorable, fun, smart, fantastic grandchildren.

Made in the USA
Monee, IL
18 December 2019

18964054R00105